Standing on the Promises

STANDING ON THE PROMISES

A Handbook of Biblical Childrearing

DOUGLAS WILSON

Canon Press

MOSCOW, IDAHO

Douglas Wilson, *Standing on the Promises: A Handbook of Biblical Childrearing*

© 1997 by Douglas Wilson,
Published by Canon Press, P.O. Box 8741, Moscow, ID 83843

02 03 04 05 06 07   11 10 9 8 7 6 5

Cover design by Paige Atwood

Printed in the United States of America.

ISBN: 1-885767-25-0

For Bekah, Nathan, and Rachel. May the Lord give you as many hours of laughter around the table with your children as He gave us with you. *Crescite et multiplicamini.*

Standing on the Promises

Table of Contents

CHAPTER ONE

A Short Overview of Covenantal Childrearing

The Fountainhead of Culture

What is a marriage? What is a family? What is a home? For many, such questions may seem ridiculous. Common sense tells us that marriage happens when two people hire a photographer to take their picture down at the church, a family is the result of children being born a little bit later, and home is where you hang your hat.

There may have been some times in history when it was safe to make assumptions about the nature of marriage and the home. Although it is doubtful, there may have been a time when the unspoken consensus about the family was adequately biblical. But whether or not this ever was the case, it is certainly not the case in our generation. In few periods of history has there been more widespread confusion about masculinity and femininity, and how these two aspects of our being were designed by God to complement each other in a biblical home, and in the biblical rearing of children.

The biblical family is an instituted government, established by God at the very beginning of human history. The constitution for this government was written by Him, and revealed to us in His Word. The head of each family is the husband, the chief advisor to this head is the wife, and the subjects of this small realm are the children. To be sure, they are temporary subjects—good parents are instructed by God to prepare their children to leave at the proper time, in order to establish their own families. Parents bring up their children to be colonists at the proper time, planting families of their own.

Consequently, each family is designed to be *a culture*—with a language, customs, traditions, and countless unspoken assumptions. God has made the world in such a way that children who grow up in the culture of the family are to be shaped and molded by it. The duty of the husband and father is to ensure that the shaping is done according to the standards of the Word of God.

But consider two possible problems. The first occurs when a husband and wife establish a very real culture in their family, but because of their sin and rebellion, it is a rebellious culture. In such a case, children are simply being brought up under the wrath of God. Unless the grace of God intervenes, the sins of the fathers are visited upon subsequent generations. The second problem, far more common among modern Christians, is that of forgetting the family is a culture at all, and allowing, by default, outside cultural influences to take primacy in how the children are shaped. When the biblical cultural mandate for the home is abandoned in the home, the vacuum will not be there for long. Because this is a fallen world, those who take over the process of shaping the children, those who rush to fill the void left by derelict husbands and disobedient wives, will always be scoundrels and fools. It is moral idiocy to leave children alone in order to let them "learn alone" or "make decisions for themselves." The fact that they are left alone by their *parents* at home does not mean they will be left alone. By nature, children are malleable. They will either be shaped lawfully, by those commanded by God to perform the task, or they will be shaped unlawfully, by outsiders. But as children, they *will* be shaped.

So the home is a culture. As Christian parents seek to apply this truth to the building of a godly culture in their families, what are some possible obstacles? The first great obstacle to overcome is within the minds of the husband

and wife themselves. The Bible tells us that we are not to be conformed to the world, but rather to be transformed through the renewing of our minds. Nowhere is it more important to break with our modern world *in our minds* than on the issue of the definition of the family. Unless true Christian culture is re-established in countless homes, it will never be re-established anywhere else. This mental obstacle within must be overcome, because most modern Christian couples have numerous unbiblical assumptions about the home.

Many couples are reluctant to assume all the responsibility for the culture and nourishment of their children. Many "cultural influences" shape our society. Parents are responsible to monitor them all. A husband must teach the Word of God to his family, especially his wife, to cleanse her with its application, encourage her when she is faint-hearted, and oversee the help she is to him. On earth, she is to be the most important person in his life, and he is to teach the children to love and honor their mom. Parents are responsible to maintain a biblical culture in the home through loving discipline, teaching and prayer, and by screening all the sinful cultivating influence coming from the outside world—whether on television, on the radio, in books, at school, or from friends.

This means that children should view the home as not simply the place where they eat and sleep, but where they are taught and shaped. They should view home as the center of their world. They should see it as their primary culture—and always view the larger culture in the light of what they have learned at home. This can be done in spite of the great obstacles. For example, the obstacle presented by television should be obvious. The "land" represented night after night on the tube is an alien culture, another land, far removed from biblical Christianity. And yet, how many Christian parents allow their children without any adequate supervision to learn their way around in this heathen culture? Because of a lack of parental oversight, how many

Christian children are video street urchins in another land? The primary concern here is *not* the "sex and violence." Those are mere symptoms of a much deeper problem, invisible to many Christian parents.

Education presents another obstacle and another example. A reactionary retreat from the government schools does not necessarily represent a biblical cultural response at all. Parents who have their children enrolled in a Christian day school are responsible to see that the cultural weight of the family is dominant in how their children are educated. This cannot be done by just dropping off the kids and tuition check. The involvement of parents must be active and it must be constant. The same care must be taken if the family is homeschooling. Abdication is possible anywhere, including a homeschooling situation with an absentee, detached father. Reaction to pagan culture is not the same as building a biblical culture. This rudimentary truth is to be first learned and applied in the home. Parents must see that their families are strengthened to the point where they become true cultures, all similar to the extent they conform to biblical standards, and all as different as their last names. Fathers must lead in establishing this biblical culture, and mothers must be convinced of the importance of it, for much of the practical implementation will be in her hands.

Receiving Little Ones

Once a husband and wife understand the vision for establishing a Christian culture in the home, they are then prepared for the privilege of receiving children from the hand of the Lord. This is important because it is a fearful thing to stumble a child—"But whoever causes one of these little ones who believe in me to sin, it would be better for him if a millstone were hung around his neck, and he were drowned in the depth of the sea" (Mt. 18:6).

The disciples had asked who was the greatest in the

kingdom of heaven. Our Lord's response made use of a nearby little one in order to show the disciples the importance of a childlike humility. The entry to the kingdom requires a conversion in childlike humility (vv. 3-4). Unless a man is so converted, he will by no means enter the kingdom of God. But having made the point about humility, the Lord continued to teach on the important subject of children—or as He states it, *little ones*. In a very real way, we can see that the kind of humility Christ was requiring here should be measured in terms of one's attitude toward children. In verse 5, He states that "whoever receives one little child like this in My name receives Me." He then utters the terrifying curse quoted above. Whoever is a stumbling block to believing little ones lies under a horrible judgment of God. In the next verse, the Lord states that the world is a sinful place and that offenses (to little ones) will come—but woe to that man through whom they come.

Of whom is He speaking? Although Christ is speaking generally, to whom do these words primarily apply? The answer is *parents*. R.L. Dabney, in an essay on parental responsibilities, makes the observation that, under God's providence, when a man and a woman have a child, they have kindled a spark that can *never* be put out. That child, blessed or cursed, will exist forever and ever. No peaceful oblivion waits for poorly-reared children. And further, God has made the world in such a way that parents have a tremendous influence over the direction their children take— either for good or evil.

How serious, then, should we as parents be in the assumption of these responsibilities? The next two verses tell us—they are the familiar ones about what we should do if our hand, foot, or eye causes us to sin. We should sacrifice them—better to enter life maimed than to be thrown into Hell whole and entire. This is still in the context of the Lord's teaching about children, for in the next verse He states, "Take heed that you do not despise one of these little ones, for I say to you that in heaven their angels always see the face of My Father who is in heaven." In other words, the Lord is teaching us that it is better to maim ourselves than to stumble our children—a very serious warning indeed.

There are three basic truths here. We as parents must be converted men and women so that we are *like* our children. We are to be teachable, humble, malleable. Secondly, we are to *receive* our children in the name of the Lord, for to do so is to receive the Lord. Pregnancy, childbearing, and child-rearing should be viewed by us with great honor, for in these things the Lord is visiting us with blessing. And lastly, we are to *take heed* that we *do not despise* our little ones.

The Lord says we are to take *heed*, take *care*, that we do not despise them. There are at least two ways to be guilty of such despising, the first being perhaps more obvious. Children are despised when they are neglected, overlooked, and shunted aside for larger, more adult concerns. It was this kind of grown-up officiousness that Christ rebuked when His disciples tried to keep the little ones away from Him (Mt. 19:14). Children matter. The Christian faith is not like those rides at Disneyland, where you have to be a certain height to participate.

But a second way of despising children is not as clear, perhaps. This happens when we *think* we are not despising them because we pay so much attention to them. We live in a culture that is obsessed with the idol of youth, but there is a vast difference between the *childlike* and teachable humility enjoined by Christ and the *childish* immaturity worshipped by MTV, Young Life, and Reebok. These words of rather severe instruction from Christ should bring us up short. When we consider the solemnity involved in the task of bringing up our children in the Lord, we should both *fear* God concerning our children and, as will be discussed in the coming chapters, *trust* God with our children.

As we bring up our children, we should descend to their level in one sense (humility) in order to lead them to our level (maturity). This is not the same as descending to their level (immaturity) in order to lead them to our level (pride). We must be servants to our children; we must *not* cater to them. One of the central problems with bringing up children in our day is the constant temptation to underestimate their capacities. We teach them profane and irreverent little ditties, not psalms and hymns. We give them moralistic little stories, not biblical doctrine and ethics. We expect them to act as though they have no brains or souls until they have graduated from college. We aim at nothing, and we hit it every time.

Foundational Assumptions for Fathers and Mothers

As children are received from the hand of the Lord, certain things must immediately follow. In order to undertake the arduous task of childrearing, every Christian parent must build on certain basic foundation stones. The first assumption is understanding that in fulfilling our parental duties and privileges, *the Bible is sufficient.* Bringing up small children can be perplexing, and will present thinking parents with many questions. But parents must remember that all questions that *need* to be answered *can* be answered from the Bible (Deut. 6:4-9; Eph. 6:4; 2 Tim. 3:16-17). Because of the Bible's sufficiency, child-psychology and counseling fads are *not* necessary.

Christian parents must also remember that *discipline is no substitute for regeneration.* Every child, no matter how cute or small or helpless is a sinner. Strict discipline may channel that sin in socially acceptable ways, but that is all it can do. Godly, strict discipline must always have a goal which goes far beyond "well-behaved kids" (Rom. 5:12,19; Eph. 2:1-3). If we are objects of wrath *by nature*, then our children share in that corruption. We are and they do. When considering age, the Bible does not contrast childish innocence and adult sinfulness. The biblical contrast is between immature sin and mature sin. The Christian parent must always take the reality of sin and rebellion into account. The fact that the children of Christian parents belong to a covenant home does not alter the reality of sin. Every child, every descendent of Adam, needs the forgiveness of Christ.

The third thing to remember is that *godly child-rearing is covenantal.* The children of believers, although they have the nature of sinners, have been given a tremendous covenantal privilege. This is the case even if only one of the parents is a believer:

> And a woman who has a husband who does not believe, if he is willing to live with her, let her not divorce him. For the unbelieving husband is sanctified by the wife, and the unbelieving wife is sanctified by the husband; otherwise your children would be unclean, but now they are holy. But if the unbeliever departs, let him depart; a brother or a sister is not under bondage in such cases. But God has called us to peace. (1 Cor. 7:13-15)

The children of unbelievers are *unclean.* The children of Christian parents are covenantally sanctified, even though their nature is not yet necessarily changed through regeneration. The fact that the child is a sinner and has not yet professed faith in Christ is grounds for watchfulness, wariness, and prayerfulness. At the same time, the covenantal sanctification of children is grounds for confidence. When all the teaching of the Bible is taken into account, parents who fulfill their covenantal obligations have every reason to *expect* that their children will be saved.

It is absolutely essential for both parents to recognize that *the final responsibility for child-rearing is the father's*—he cannot pass it off to the wife. The husband must lead his wife in child-rearing. He must not react to her, he must not blame her, and he must not be led by her. This is what headship necessarily involves. The husband is the head of his wife (Eph. 5:23), and he is responsible for all the fruit she bears (Eph. 6:4). It is crucial that this responsibility of the husband be *embraced* by him and understood by her.

Parents must also remember that *young children are not equipped for independence.* If parents do well in the first five years, then they will be spared much grief later. Grown children are to be fully independent (Gen. 2:24; Eph. 5:31). Older children at home are obviously to be quasi-independent, as the parents prepare them for the time they leave. But young children are *dependent.* Many parents try to reverse this order. If parents look for undirected spontaneity in their young children, all they will get is spontaneous sin. Christian parents are to be involved; watching children grow to maturity is not a spectator sport.

Leadership in Childrearing

Leadership necessarily involves *initiative.* Many men have blurred the (admittedly fine) distinction between being the head of the home and being a queen bee. A slug on the sofa may be waited on, but he is *not* exercising godly leadership. In Ephesians 5:25, and 6:4, the verbs *love* and *bring up* are active verbs. In the home, the husband is a picture of Christ. But if he shows no initiative in loving, teaching, or admonishing, he is a *lying* picture of Christ. In other words, each husband, every day, is talking about Christ through his behavior. What he says is either a truth or a lie, but he cannot be silent. So masculine initiative means watching over the family without prompting, and it means seeking information about the children from the wife *at his instigation*.

Leadership also involves honoring and respecting a wife's limitations. The principle is found in 1 Peter 3:7—"Husbands, likewise, dwell with them with understanding, giving honor to the wife, as to the weaker vessel, and as being heirs together of the grace of life, that your prayers may not be hindered." The application should be obvious in bringing up little ones. Generally, children are far more mindful of their father than their mother. But childrearing is not a competition; it is not a foot race between father and mother. The man and his wife are on the *same team*. The fact that the children don't mind their mother as readily should be understood by the husband, and he must always back her up. Whenever children are looking at their mother, they should see the looming shadow of dad behind her—whether he's home or not.

Leadership in childrearing also involves honoring and respecting a woman's strengths and dignity. In Genesis 1:28, God gives mankind the job of being fruitful, multiplying, filling the earth and subduing it. But this was not a job that Adam could do alone. God said it was not good for him to be alone (Gen. 2:18). In the task of bringing up children, the help the wife brings is not just in the area of biological reproduction. She is given to her husband in order to help him *bring them up*. He therefore needs her perspective; he needs her wisdom. Because God wants godly offspring (Mal. 2:15), the husband must therefore keep covenant with the wife of his youth (Mal. 2:13-16).

However unpleasant it may appear to the flesh, godly leadership necessarily involves sacrifice. Jesus taught us that the way to be a godly leader involves servanthood. Who is the master of the sheep? The shepherd, obviously. But who is the servant to the sheep? The answer is equally obvious.

In the same way, who is the master of a newborn? And who is the servant? Parents have full authority, but it is the authority of servanthood. Husbands have full authority, but it is the authority of servanthood. "And He sat down, called the twelve, and said to them, 'If anyone desires to be first, he shall be last of all and servant of all'" (Mk. 9:35). A man who wants to be first in his home (and every man should) must pursue that position the way Christ instructed. He should want to have authority in the home, for he was appointed to that position. But what method has Christ required him to follow in order to get there? The answer is *service*. A husband and wife must, through example and words, see that discipline is for the benefit of the children, and not for the benefit of the one disciplining. The children must understand this principle as well. Consequently, in the home, it is wrong to allow discipline that is not *entirely calm*.

Children in Our Midst

Speaking of the time when the Messiah would reign over His people, Ezekiel says that "they shall dwell there, they, their children, and their children's children, forever; and My servant David shall be their prince forever" (Ezek. 37:25). We are taught in Genesis and Ephesians that "a man shall leave his father and mother and be joined to his wife, and the two shall become one flesh" (Eph. 5:31). But why did God establish marriage in this way? "He seeks godly offspring" (Mal. 2:15).

As will be discussed in the following chapters, the Bible teaches us that the norm for faithful members of the covenant is that their children will follow them in their faithfulness. "The children of Your servants will continue, and their descendants will be established before You" (Ps. 102:28). As Christians, we should know that "the mercy of the Lord is from everlasting to everlasting on those who fear Him, and His righteousness to children's children, to such as keep His covenant, and to those who remember His commandments to do them" (Ps. 103:17-18). The Lord's mother held this last promise close to her heart (Lk. 1:50).

Of course this does not teach automatic transfer of saving grace to our children. If we disobey the terms of the covenant—especially with regard to the way we train our children—then we have no right to be dismayed with the result. The biblical facts are plain. The Bible is full of promises to parents. But the promises are for those parents who are in the covenant, keep the covenant, and remember His commandments to do them. In other words, parents who do as they are commanded may comfort themselves with the words of Scripture: "My elect shall long enjoy the work of their hands. They shall not labor in vain, nor bring forth children for trouble; for they shall be the descendants of the blessed of the Lord, and their offspring with them" (Is. 65:22b-23).

One of the reasons we fail to comfort ourselves with these promises is that we are reluctant to assume the converse responsibility for failure. But the Bible addresses this as well. Parents within the covenant can fail to fulfill their covenantal duties with regard to their children (Prov. 29:15). Why is it a shame for parents to have a disobedient child? Such parents are ashamed because they have everything to do with the existence of that disobedience. This is a conclusion we hesitate to draw, and consequently the promised blessing of covenantal succession for faithful parents is missed.

Some may object and say that this is a burden that no fallen parent can bear—who is sufficient for these things? The answer of course is that in ourselves none of us is sufficient. But these promises were given, not to the angels, but to *us*. The angels could be perfect parents, except they are not parents. The promises of the covenant are given to forgiven sinners. And because they are gospel promises they are ours by grace through faith. Christian parents should anticipate seeing their children grow up knowing the Lord. This should not be seen as an oddity—the oddity should be children who fall away. And of course the conversion experiences of crack addicts who previously rode with the Hell's Angels should not be used as the conversion paradigm for children who have grown up in godly, nurturing homes.

In Ephesians 6:4, fathers are told to bring up their children in the education and admonition of the Lord. These fathers are not commanded to attempt a distinction between elect and non-elect children. Christian fathers are commanded to bring up *all* the children born into their homes in this fashion. And the process is His because the children are His. Transgenerational blessing is assumed throughout the Bible. Peter says that the promise is to "you and to your children, and to all who are afar off, as many as the Lord our God will call" (Acts 2:39). It is quite true this is governed by the divine will—as many as the Lord our God will call—but given the copious and clear teaching of the Old Testament, and Peter's reference to it, there is no reason to believe the Lord wants to be miserly in His grace. For covenantally faithful parents, because the promise of Scripture cannot be broken, the Lord's gracious calling of our children, grandchildren, and great-grandchildren is something in which we can rest. A detailed discussion of these great covenantal promises and their related duties should therefore be our delight.

CHAPTER TWO

The Promises of God to Parents

Throughout the Scriptures, God has given many promises to those parents who fear Him. From the beginning, biblical child-rearing in the light of these promises has been covenantal. As we have seen, godly offspring are sought by God in the homes of His people as the result of a godly marriage *covenant*. "But did He not make them one, having a remnant of the Spirit? And why one? He seeks godly offspring. Therefore take heed to your spirit, and let none deal treacherously with the wife of his youth" (Mal 2:15). In the previous verse the wife was described as a "wife by *covenant*." Marriage is a covenantal union, designed by God with a set purpose in mind—and that purpose is a *fruitful* covenantal union. God designed biblical marriage with the intention of bringing godly offspring into the world.

Now it is true that a marriage can exist apart from the covenantal redemption that we have in Christ—non-Christians marry—and are obligated to fulfill their vows. But marriage does not exist *as God requires in His Word* unless the marriage covenant is set in the context of the *redemptive* covenant that we have in Christ. In other words, there is no way to honor the marriage covenant properly without a larger covenantal submission and obedience in view.

Now the Scriptures are equally clear that the heart of *covenant-keeping* is *promise-believing*. This is why the Bible, from beginning to end, teaches the centrality of faith. But as it was with Abraham, promise-believing, or faith, without works is dead. Nowhere is this more important to understand than in the arduous task of bringing up our children in the Lord. To keep us from being overwhelmed by our responsibilities as parents, we must turn first to the promises of God that apply to us as parents. It is a tragedy of monumental proportions that most modern Christian parents are not aware of the wonderful promises that God has made in His Word on the subject of child-rearing. But as we come to understand these promises, we will then *rest* in them, and that evangelical rest will result in godly, trusting, faithful parental *work*.

Old Testament Promises

"The *children of Your servants* will continue, and their descendants will be established before You" (Ps. 102:28). This is a promise to parents that is based on the unchanging character of God. In the previous verses the psalmist has said, "Of old You laid the foundation of the earth, and the heavens are the work of Your hands. They will perish, but You will endure; yes, they will all grow old like a garment; like a cloak You will change them, and they will be changed. But You are the same, and Your years will have no end" (Ps. 102:25-27).

Because God does not change over generations, He can sustain the descendants of His servants. But this is not merely a statement about God's *abilities*; it is a promise concerning His *intentions*. We are not told here what God can do; we are told what He will do. And this unchanging purpose is based squarely on His unchanging character.

This intention of God's is also seen in the Ten Commandments—"You shall not bow down to them nor serve them. For I, the LORD your God, am a jealous God, visiting the iniquity of the fathers *upon the children* to the third and fourth generations of those who hate Me, but showing mercy to thousands, to those who love Me and keep My commandments" (Deut. 5:9-10). The implication here is that blessings flow to thousands of *generations*. With regard to the effect of iniquity, He has spoken of three and four generations, and then turns to speak of thousands. Thousands of what? The plain meaning is thousands of generations. And we have further support for this understanding:

> Therefore know that the LORD your God, He is God, the faithful God who keeps covenant and mercy for a thousand generations with those who love Him and keep His commandments. (Deut. 7:9)

This passage is just a few chapters after the Ten Commandments and clearly echoes the language of the Decalogue. But two additional and important features should be noted as well. First, it spells out God's intention of blessing to a thousand *generations*. Secondly, it says that this is the result of a faithful God *keeping covenant* with families.

The paradigm for this is Abraham—the father of all who believe.

> And I will establish My covenant between Me and you and your descendants after you in their generations, for an everlasting covenant, to be God to you and your descendants after you. Also I give to you and your descendants after you the land in which you are a stranger, all the land of Canaan, as an everlasting possession; and I will be their God." And God said to Abraham: "As for you, you shall keep My covenant, you and your descendants after you throughout their generations. (Gen. 17:7-9)

God made an everlasting covenant with Abraham, and with his descendants after him. This covenant contained, and still contains, two elements. The first, and most important, is "I will be your God." Not only does He promise to be

Abraham's God, He says that He will be God to Abraham's *descendants*. The second promise here is that He will give to Abraham and his descendants the land of Canaan. This latter portion of the promise has been physically fulfilled, but this does not mean that the fullness of the promise has been exhausted. Paul teaches that the promises concerning the land of Canaan are still in force, although under the New Covenant they have been greatly expanded—

> For the promise that he would be the heir of the world was not to Abraham or to his seed through the law, but through the righteousness of faith. (Rom. 4:13)

The promise to Abraham still stands, and the promise to his seed is still set before us. The change is that God is now giving us the *world* instead of just the land of Canaan This change or expansion of the covenant is in no way the result of faithlessness on God's part. Suppose a man made an agreement with his son that if he mowed the lawn he would be given five dollars. If the son mowed the lawn and then was given two dollars, *that* would be faithlessness on the father's part. But if he gives him one hundred dollars, there is obviously no faithlessness at all. This is what God has done for us. He made a covenant with Abraham and his descendants. The New Covenant is not the result of God scrapping the covenant with Abraham; it is the fulfillment of God's covenant with Abraham. Because it is such an *expansive* fulfillment, it does *not* exclude our children.

Does it automatically include them then? Certainly not. If parents are not covenantally faithful in how they bring up their children, and if their children do not embrace the faith of Abraham their father, the genetic relationship alone does no good at all. Any who live and die in unbelief are of their father the devil. *God can make sons of Abraham out of rocks* (Mt. 3:9). But we see in these passages (and it is a glorious truth) that God can also make sons of Abraham out of sons of Abraham. What is more, He has declared His intention to do so.

Old Testament Predictions

In the Old Testament, we are not limited to promises made to the Old Testament saints. It is very clear throughout the Old Testament that the church of God was in its nonage. But a time was coming, as the prophets knew and declared, when the promises would be fulfilled and realized in a glorious way. A mark of how little we understand the Bible is that modern Christians have come to understand the New Testament era as that time when God abrogated His earlier promises, and started over from scratch, rather than the time when God fulfilled His promises in a glorious way.

The promises in the Old Testament of the Christian era, the Christian *aeon*, are indeed glorious. Moreover, these promises are not silent on the subject of the children of *Christians*. "David My servant shall be king over them, and they shall all have one shepherd; they shall also walk in My judgments and observe My statutes, and do them. Then they shall dwell in the land that I have given to Jacob My servant, where your fathers dwelt; and they shall dwell there, *they, their children, and their children's children, forever*; and My servant David shall be their prince forever. Moreover I will make a covenant of peace with them, and it shall be an everlasting covenant with them; I will establish them and multiply them, and I will set My sanctuary in their midst forevermore" (Ezek. 37:24-26). Ezekiel is talking about the time when David (the Christ, who was the son of David) shall reign. Notice how this is a prophecy of a great *expansion* of generational blessings. When Christ reigns, whom shall He rule? He shall rule them, their *children*, and their *grandchildren*, and He shall do so *forever*. Not only do these blessings cross generational lines, they do so again on the basis of an everlasting covenant. In other words, Ezekiel predicts that in the gospel era children and grandchildren and great-grandchildren will be brought up in the Lord. Note that this is not something that might or might not happen. God promises that it *will* happen.

This is also predicted in Isaiah's great millennial prophecy. Notice how Isaiah speaks of this.

> They shall not build and another inhabit; they shall not plant and another eat; for as the days of a tree, so shall be the days of My people, and My elect shall long enjoy the work of their hands. They shall not labor in vain, nor bring forth children for trouble; for they shall be the descendants of the blessed of the LORD, *and their offspring with them.* (Is. 65:23)

As a result of Christ's work on the cross, His people shall no longer bring forth children for trouble—they and their descendants shall be the blessed of the Lord. When shall this be? It will not be after the final resurrection of the dead—at that time we will no longer marry or be given in marriage. We will not rear children in heaven. This is a prophecy that will be fulfilled during of the era of gospel. In other words, these are promises that apply to *us*, and as the Christian *aeon* progresses, the fulfillment of these promises will become more and more manifest.

There is another wonderful promise very much like this just a few chapters earlier in Isaiah. Again, it is a promise concerning the gospel era. Isaiah is talking about our day, and the days to come. "As for Me," says the LORD, "this is My covenant with them: My Spirit who is upon you, and My words which I have put in your mouth, shall not depart from your mouth, nor from the mouth of your *descendants*, nor from the mouth of your *descendants' descendants*," says the LORD, "from this time and forevermore" (Is. 59:21). What does this mean? This simply means that God did not abandon His commitment to generations in the four hundred years between Malachi and Matthew.

At all times, in all ages, our God remains a covenant-keeping God. As such a God, He delights to keep covenant with families across generations.

New Testament Confirmation

Not only do the saints in the Old Testament look forward in expectation to the fulfillment of such wonderful promises, the saints in the pages of the New Testament look *back* at the promises. And what is very important, they teach us how we are to think, as Christians, about these promises.

> But the mercy of the LORD is from everlasting to everlasting on those who fear Him, and His righteousness *to children's children*, to such as keep His covenant, and to those who remember His commandments to do them.
> (Ps. 103:17-18)

This promise is stated as "everlasting." Now some believe that the transition from the Levitical administration to the New Covenant somehow sets aside such "everlastings." However, Mary, our Lord's mother, thought very differently about it. Notice how she refers to this passage from Psalm 103 in her psalm of praise.

> For He has regarded the lowly state of His maidservant; for behold, henceforth all generations will call me blessed. For He who is mighty has done great things for me, and holy is His name. And His mercy is on those who fear Him *from generation to generation.* (Lk. 1:48-50)

Notice also how Mary uses the term "generation." She does not believe that the Messiah to be born of her is coming to earth to introduce some new approach to the generations of God's people. It is not as though God were somehow concerned for the preservation of generations in the Old Testament, but now, in the New Testament

He begins to say, "Every man for himself!" The arrival of the Messiah is a demonstration of God's faithfulness *to* the generations of His people; it is *not* the point at which He abandons them. The mother of the Messiah knows this, and affirms it.

We also see this understanding in Paul's treatment of the family in Ephesians 5:31.

> For this reason a man shall leave his father and mother and be joined to his wife, and the two shall become one flesh." This is a great mystery, but I speak concerning Christ and the church. Nevertheless let each one of you in particular so love his own wife as himself, and let the wife see that she respects her husband. Children, obey your parents in the Lord, for this is right. "Honor your father and mother," which is the first commandment with promise: "that it may be well with you and you may live long on the earth." And you, fathers, do not provoke your children to wrath, but bring them up in the training and admonition of the Lord. (Eph. 5:31-6:4)

Paul is addressing *Gentile* parents here, and he expressly tells them about a promise from the Ten Commandments which he says applies to them. The only problem is that it is a promise *originally* made to the Jews at Mount Sinai concerning their occupation of the land of Canaan. God had told them that if they honored their fathers and mothers it would go well for them in the *land*. And with the same wonderful liberty we saw earlier, Paul here expands the blessing of the promise—the promise now includes *Gentiles*, and it encompasses the *earth*.

It is important for us to realize the context of these words to parents. Paul is not speaking to generic Christians. He is speaking to Gentiles; earlier in this same letter he had emphasized their adoption *into Israel*, and their wonderful inclusion into the covenants of promise. This adoption into Israel is why the promise in the Decalogue applies to Gentiles. *It would not apply to them otherwise.*

The passage is worth quoting at length.

> Therefore remember that you, once Gentiles in the flesh—
> who are called Uncircumcision by what is called the Cir-
> cumcision made in the flesh by hands—that at that time
> you were without Christ, being aliens from the common-
> wealth of Israel and *strangers from the covenants of prom-
> ise*, having no hope and without God in the world. But now
> in Christ Jesus you who once were far off have been
> brought near by the blood of Christ. For He Himself is
> our peace, who has made both one, and has broken down
> the middle wall of separation, having abolished in His flesh
> the enmity, that is, the law of commandments contained
> in ordinances, so as to create in Himself one new man from
> the two, thus making peace, and that He might reconcile
> them both to God in one body through the cross, thereby
> putting to death the enmity. And He came and preached
> peace to you who were afar off and to those who were
> near. For through Him we both have access by one Spirit
> to the Father. Now, therefore, you are no longer strang-
> ers and foreigners, but fellow citizens with the saints and
> members of the household of God, having been built on
> the foundation of the apostles and prophets, Jesus Christ
> Himself being the chief corner stone, in whom the whole
> building, being joined together, grows into a holy temple
> in the Lord, in whom you also are being built together for
> a dwelling place of God in the Spirit. (Eph. 2:11-22)

Gentiles have now been included into Israel. On what
basis? On that of circumcision? Obviously not. Where
once stood Jew and Gentile, circumcised and uncircum-
cised, now stands one new man—the Christian man. Christians are those who possess one Lord, one faith, one
baptism (Eph. 4:5). Gentiles once were outside the commonwealth of Israel; now they are citizens of Israel. Note
that it is their baptism which declares their membership
in this Renewed Israel. Once they were strangers to the
covenants of promise contained in the Old Testament—
now they are blessed as recipients of these covenants. But

what do these covenants promise? What promise is being given to the Gentiles here? It is the same promise given to Abraham—it is the great and central promise of the covenant. *You will be My people, and I will be your God.* It would be truly bizarre if Paul were telling them that Gentiles were now included in the covenant, and now had the promises, but then forbade them to look at what the promises contained in that covenant actually said. The content of the promises emphasizes, time and time again, the spiritual well-being of our children.

The conclusion is inescapable. A prominent feature of faithful covenantal thinking in the Old Testament is the *salvation* of offspring. The New Testament echoes this language. In Ephesians the promise concerning well-being of descendants from the Decalogue is expressly applied to believing Gentiles. This is done on the basis of the inclusion of Gentiles *into Israel* and *into the covenant*. It is commonly assumed that the covenant with Abraham's "seed" merely gave them the right to be called physical Jews, as opposed to being called Hittites. Now these glorious promises have certainly been distorted and misapplied to and by nominalistic Jews, just as the New Covenant form of the same promises has been distorted and misapplied to and by nominalistic Christians.

But we must not measure covenantal truth by those who are *faithless* to the covenant. In order to determine what is true, we are to look to the Word, and not to people. What does *God* say about those who are covenantally faithful? What does He say about their children? Their grandchildren? Does He *promise* anything concerning them? The answer is *yes*.

In this light, and in this context, the words of Peter in his sermon at Pentecost take on a new significance. He is preaching to Jews who have been thinking generationally for over a millennium. Does this new teaching, this gospel, introduce an atomization of God's promises? Not at all, Peter says "the promise is to you and *your children*"

(Acts 2:39). In the verses immediately preceding, in response to their convicted inquiry, Peter has told his audience what they need to do.

> Now when they heard this, they were cut to the heart, and said to Peter and the rest of the apostles, "Men and brethren, what shall we do?" Then Peter said to them, "Repent, and let every one of you be baptized in the name of Jesus Christ for the remission of sins; and you shall receive the gift of the Holy Spirit. For the promise is to you and to your children, and to all who are afar off, as many as the Lord our God will call." (Acts 2:37-39)

Notice the elements here. The gospel is preached. Men are convicted and cry out, wondering what their response should be. Peter tells them to repent, and he tells them to be baptized. Why? He tells them to do so because the gift of the Holy Spirit awaits—for the *promise* (there's that word again!) is to them and to their *children*. Now what are these children doing here? They are invited by the promises of God all through the Old Testament—promises of the coming Holy Spirit, poured out at Pentecost. The Spirit was not portioned out with a teaspoon; He was *poured* out. And as we look forward to an ever-increasing fulfillment of His ministry and work in our world, we can expect (because God has promised it) the restoration of all things. The Holy Spirit will efficaciously and sovereignly regenerate countless *generations*.

With assurances like this, we can truly rejoice that our God is a covenant-keeping God. "For the LORD is good; His mercy is everlasting, and His truth endures to all generations" (Ps. 100:5).

CHAPTER THREE

The Duties of Parents Before God

The promises of God discussed in the last chapter are indeed glorious; they provide true comfort. At the same time, such promises naturally generate questions. Do these promises mean that the children of believers are *automatically* going to heaven? Are the children of elect parents automatically elect themselves? A thoughtful reading of Scripture indicates otherwise—not to mention a brief glance at the experience of some of our Christian friends.

Whenever we are engaged in a trying and difficult task, such as parenting, we commonly need encouragement. This is why the promises we have discussed are so important. As parents, we care very much about the results of our labor; and as we labor, we need to rely on the promises of God. Labor without encouragement from the promises is self-righteous legalism, and claiming promises without labor is nothing but foolish presumption. The heart of covenant-keeping is promise-believing—and faith without works is dead.

We must therefore consider the duties established for parents in the Word. As we considered the promises of God to parents, our first thought perhaps was that they are too good to be true. But as we meditate upon them, we should come to realize that our duty is to *believe* these promises. This leads us to ask, what does such evangelical belief look like? How does it appear in the world? Faith, in Scripture, is always manifested in works. Faith does not stand alone, nor do works stand alone. Neither do we work in order to attain faith. Faith is given as a *gift*, and when it is given by God, it appears to the world in the form of *fruit*. In the case of our children, the fruit is diligent and careful parenting.

Obedience to the Mercy of the Lord

"But the mercy of the LORD is from everlasting to everlasting on those who fear Him, and His righteousness to children's children, *to such as keep His covenant*, and to *those who remember His commandments* to *do* them" (Ps. 103:17-18). The promise in this passage is clear. But three elements of parental responsibility also need to be mentioned—*keeping* the covenant, *remembering* His commandments, and *doing* His commandments.

First we should consider what it means to keep His covenant. The heart of all biblical covenant-keeping is *trust* in the promises of God. Remember how the Bible describes the covenant that was made with Abraham: "And I will establish My covenant between Me and you and your descendants after you in their generations, for an everlasting covenant, to be God to you and your descendants after you" (Gen. 17:7). But what was it that put Abraham right with God?—"For what does the Scripture say? 'Abraham believed God, and it was accounted to him for righteousness'" (Rom. 4:3). So the center of keeping God's covenant with regard to childrearing is to understand and believe the kinds of passages that were addressed in the previous chapter.

But the psalmist goes on to say that we are to *remember* His commandments, and we are to *do* them. The promises of God are annexed to His commandments. We must be very careful here. It is very easy to distort the biblical order of *faith* and *works*, as well as the relationship between them. Believing God always results in faithful obedience to Him. We must never seek to start with faithful obedience. Nowhere is it more important to have the theology of *justification* and *sanctification* straight than here on the subject of child-rearing. We are justified by faith in the promise of God, manifested in our initial trust. We are sanctified by faith in the promise of God, manifested in our on-going obedience. We are set free to walk through the process of sanctification because we have been fully and completely justified by faith *alone*—"That the righteous requirement of the law might be fulfilled in us who do not walk according to the flesh but according to the Spirit" (Rom. 8:4).

The well-worn cliche of a cart and horse is probably almost as old as the debate over faith and works, but it may still help us understand the relationship between them. Faith in God and His Word is the horse that pulls the entire cart. The cart is the work that follows as a result. This is not complicated, but sin regularly distorts the truth of it anyway. The legalist tries to pull the horse in the cart, and the antinomian shoots the horse and burns the cart. The Christian does neither.

But simply having the relationship between justification and sanctification straight is not sufficient. We still have to know what the standards of sanctification *are*, and what they are for parents. We have to *remember* and *do*. There are many instructions for parents throughout Scripture, but three of the more basic duties may be briefly indentified.

1. Personal obedience yourself—"Fathers, do not provoke your children, lest they become discouraged" (Col. 3:21). In a Christian home, the children are under the authority of parents who are under authority themselves. Nothing undermines godly parenting more than hypocrisy. When children see that they are expected to be obedient to the parents' authority while the parents have no such expectation for themselves, the results are regularly disastrous.

2. Intercession for your children—

So it was, when the days of feasting had run their course, that Job would send and sanctify them, and he would rise early in the morning and offer burnt offerings according to the number of them all. For Job said, "It may be that my sons have sinned and cursed God in their hearts." Thus Job did regularly. (Job 1:5)

As the context makes clear, Job was righteous in what he was doing. Not only did Job pray for his children, he did so as their *representative*. Our modern mentality is that the home is simply a traditional cultural system for organizing roommates. But Job did not pray for his children because he *liked* them, or because he was close to them. He prayed because he was responsible. He offered sacrifice for *their* sin.

3. Instruction in God's standards—

Hear, O Israel: The LORD our God, the LORD is one! You shall love the LORD your God with all your heart, with all your soul, and with all your strength. And these words which I command you today shall be in your heart. You shall teach them diligently to your children, and shall talk of them when you sit in your house, when you walk by the way, when you lie down, and when you rise up. You shall bind them as a sign on your hand, and they shall be as frontlets between your eyes. You shall write them on the doorposts of your house and on your gates. (Deut. 6:4-9)

We must notice that the greatest commandment is given to us in the context of a passage on bringing up our children with a Christian education. Parents are to teach their children the law of God, and they are to do so without ceasing. We see here a life-style of teaching the standards of God.

When we consider how many parents today abdicate this responsibility for teaching their children, with the task then taken up by unbelieving government schools, day care centers, television sets, radios, and so forth, it is not surprising that such parents can take no comfort from the promises of God. James tells us that to hear the Word without actual performance is a form of self-deception. "But be doers of the word, and not hearers only, deceiving yourselves" (Jas. 1:22). Understanding the biblical standards of parenting is useless without obedience. Christian parents must begin *doing* these things, and to do them in a consistent fashion.

Faith and Works

The promises of God for parents are indeed glorious. But as we see when we consider the resultant faithful performance of parental duties, the promises are not given to every name in the phone directory. Nor are they given to every name in the *church* directory. There is a very close correlation between those parents with the promises, and those parents who fulfill their God-ordained parental responsibilities. But we must remember the relationship between promises and duties in general. Only through understanding this relationship will the performance of our duty, in any area, remain *evangelical*.

As mentioned above, this area of parental responsibility is simply a small portion of the larger question concerning faith and works, conversion and perseverance. Those who maintain a high standard of biblical holiness as a biblical necessity must insist, with equal strength, that all true holiness is built upon the foundation of the absolute and efficacious grace of God. As discussed above, the promises of God never rest upon our performance of our duty in any way. Rather the performance of our duty rests upon the faithfulness of God. Indeed, the godly performance of those who believe is *one of the things promised*.

But how are we to identify those to whom the   promises are given? The biblical answer is uniform—*we recognize them by their fruit.* We identify those to whom the promises are given by seeing those who have *received* the fulfillment of the promises. God's promises never fall to the ground. When He makes promises concerning children, He keeps those promises.

As parents, we must not do our duty in order to earn our way into the promises. The promises of God are freely given in Christ to all parents who believe them. And how can we recognize who they are who so believe? They are the ones who believe the promises in such a way that it results in a glad, joyful, evangelical performance of their parental duties—which in turn results in the promised fruit. God does not transform a thornbush into an apple tree because it was producing so many fine apples the way it was before. He, by a work of His grace, makes the change which is afterwards seen and recognized. And how is it seen? It is seen in the *apples*.

As we turn to the many responsibilities that Scriptures place on faithful parents, it is important to keep this truth in mind. Otherwise, we will be overwhelmed because here, as elsewhere, the law of God is perfect and we are not. God does not call us to a job of parenting that is somehow "in the ballpark." He calls us to covenantal faithfulness. As we look at these requirements, it will be borne in on us yet again that we are all sinners, and that we all need the forgiveness of Christ constantly. At the same time, by the grace of God, covenantal faithfulness remains within reach—even for forgiven sinners.

Commands to Parents

We begin with the express commands of God to parents. Some of the commands are just presented as commands, while others are attached to God's promised response.

In order to have a garden full of weeds, it is not necessary to do anything. One must just let it go. And in order to have a home full of grief, it is not necessary to do anything either. Just let it go. God clearly instructs parents on what they should do to prevent this from happening. "Correct your son, and he will give you rest; yes, he will give delight to your soul" (Prov. 29:17). If a man corrects his son in the way this verse instructs, the result will be that the son gives rest and delight to the father. If the father does not have this rest and delight, it is because he did not correct his son the way he was instructed. The disobedience of the son toward his father is simply a small picture of the disobedience of the father toward the Father.

There are many parents who do not discipline their children the way they ought to. Commonly this is the result of a false tenderheartedness—the father hates the thought of the pain that such correction brings. He refrains from discipline because he thinks he is loving his son. The Bible says differently. "He who spares his rod hates his son, but he who loves him disciplines him promptly" (Prov. 13:24). A man who does not spank his son hates his son. This does not mean that he is filled with emotional revulsion for his son. It means that the lack of discipline has a destructive impact on the future course of that son's life. A parental refusal to discipline is therefore an act of hatred.

What is important to note is that Scripture teaches that lack of discipline has consequences. Whether or not the children of Christians "turn out" is not the result of some archangel spinning a cosmic roulette wheel. How our children do in life is the result of how we taught and disciplined them in our homes. "Chasten your son while there is hope, and do not set your heart on his destruction" (Prov. 19:18). Parents who do not chasten their children at the right time are passing by the moment of opportunity—"while there is hope." Refusal to chasten a son at this time is the same thing as setting one's heart on his destruction. Parents who do not discipline their children according to God's Word *are attempting to destroy their children*. By the grace and mercy of God, sometimes such attempts fail, but it is only by the grace of God. Parents who intervene through godly discipline are promised by God that such discipline will bear the appropriate fruit at the time of harvest. Discipline is an act of love which will save children from destruction. This, too, is only by the grace of God.

"Foolishness is bound up in the heart of a child; the rod of correction will drive it far from him" (Prov. 22:15). God does not say that the rod of discipline will pound the foolishness of a child into a seething resentment. He does not say that the rod of discipline will provoke a child to anger. He says that the rod, biblically applied, will *remove foolishness* from a child. This is obviously not to be taken in isolation from the other duties of parents, but at the same time, God promises to act through proper parental discipline. When He does not act in this way, it is because the *parents* are being disobedient and are neglecting to do what God commanded in the home.

The Word of God is not at all ambiguous on this. As parents, we are told what to do, and we are also told what happens *when* we do. "Train up a child in the way he should go, and when he is old he will not depart from it" (Prov. 22:6). Now obviously biblical training consists of far more than spanking. Parents are told to teach their children the terms of God's law, and they are told to do so all the time. "And these words which I command you today shall be in your heart. You shall teach them diligently to your children. . ." (Deut. 6:6-7). Children of Christian parents are to be brought up in an environment dominated by the Word of God. Parents are to be diligent in teaching their children the law of God all the time. When the children are not present with the parents (say, at school), the parents are still responsible for what the children are being taught in their absence. If the children are watching the tube, the parents are responsible for what is being taught. The teaching the children receive is to be comprehensive and godly.

This does not change in the New Testament. We see full continuity between the Old and New Testament on the subject of faithful parenting. The same expectation of parental oversight under the New Covenant continues on from the Old. In Ephesians 6:4 Paul tells fathers something very significant. "And you, fathers, do not provoke your children to wrath, but bring them up in the training and admonition of the Lord" (Eph. 6:4). Children of Christian parents are to be brought up in the education and admonition of the Lord. The word translated "training" in this verse is *paideia*—it refers to far more than an occasional Sunday School class. It is the *education of the Lord*. Now this kind of teaching, coupled with the consistent loving discipline mentioned above, is the instrument which God uses to raise up a godly seed within the covenant community. But when the members of that covenant community begin to think that the privileges of the covenant are *automatically* transmitted, the result is always "sons of Abraham" who are really sons of the devil—circumcision, baptism, and choir membership notwithstanding.

As the verses above make clear, there are no promises to parents who are simply "nice people," well-liked by all their friends at church. All the friends at church mean only that there will be plenty of people around to sympathize when a child destroys his life. The promises are not to those who are decent enough to get along with others. The promises are to those parents who believe God in the home, and who consequently diligently perform what they were told to do in the home. Another way to say this is that we have redefined the phrase "good parents" to suit our liking. And because we all know "good parents" by *our* definition who have children far away from the Lord, we think that God has therefore made no promises to "good parents." But He has—to those parents who have obeyed His Word in the home.

In our culture, parents will excuse themselves by saying things like, "We did everything we could." In the first place, no sinner ever has the right to say anything like this—no one of us has ever done *everything* he could. Secondly, the claim is not only false, it is glaringly false. The children were not taught to pray by their parents, they were not taught the Word by their parents, they were educated by priests of Baal down at the local government school, and they were not biblically corrected and chastised by their parents. The fact that we continue to be surprised at the results of our parental disobedience and neglect is the real problem.

Parental Shame

Kindness can kill. We see this among Christians when some grieved parents are struggling with a wayward son or daughter. The natural (and *appropriate*) reaction on the part of the parents to this backsliding of children is embarrassment and shame.

But because Christians hate to see anyone in any distress at all, they frequently seek to help with *a false and lying comfort*. The parents may be saying, perhaps for the first time in their lives, "This is all our fault." Their friends hasten to comfort them by saying things like, "But this could happen to anyone. You were good parents. Don't blame yourself like that." It appears that our modern self-centered age has finally settled upon what we think the greatest commandment should have been—"Thou shalt feel good about thyself." Absolutely nothing can be permitted to interfere with this newfangled duty—not even failure in the most important duty that God has ever given to mortal men and women. Sadly, this assumption has crept into the church.

But the reaction of shame by many parents in such a situation is proper and correct. The Scriptures teach a direct connection between how children are brought up and how they turn out. When God-fearing parents are confronted with a God-defying child, shame is an entirely appropriate response. In this shame the parents are acknowledging that they are responsible for what has happened.

This truth is seen all through the book of Proverbs. Sinful behavior on the part of children is a disgrace and a shame to their *parents*. We can begin with a verse which shows the correlation between shame and a lack of appropriate discipline. "The rod and rebuke give wisdom, but a child left to himself brings shame to his mother" (Prov. 29:15). When children are disciplined the way God requires, the result is wisdom. When children are neglected in discipline, the result is shame. Why shame? The results would have been different had the behavior of the parents been different.

But mothers are not singled out. When a man's son begins running with the wrong crowd, it is a shame to his father. Notice that the father is not said to be *concerned* about his son's friends, but rather *shamed* by them. "Whoever keeps the law is a discerning son, but a companion of gluttons shames his father" (Prov. 28:7). The same is true of laziness. Children are not just to be disciplined for bad behavior, they are to be trained and disciplined in the joys and rewards of hard work. If they are not, it is a shame to the parents. "He who gathers in summer is a wise son; he who sleeps in harvest is a son who causes shame" (Prov. 10:5). But why should *one* man be ashamed of the laziness of *another*? The answer is that, as a father, he is *responsible* for it. The son should have been taught to love honest work, and he was not taught.

Another area where many parents fail is in their refusal to insist that the children treat them with the proper respect. Parents hesitate at this point because they think this is somehow self-exalting. But parents are required to bring their children up in all the laws of God, and one of the most basic of these laws is the requirement to honor father and mother. Who is to teach and instill this, if the father and mother do not? Failure to do so, not surprisingly, results in shame. "He who mistreats his father and chases away his mother is a son who causes shame and brings reproach" (Prov. 19:26). The shame that results from parental failure is not just a temporary embarrassment. In many cases, it can cause the dissolution of a family, interfere with the rights of inheritance, and more. "A wise servant will rule over a son who causes shame, and will share an inheritance among the brothers" (Prov. 17:2).

When Christians encourage parents with a false comfort, the shame is not really removed. It does, however, put a whitewash over it, which causes a good deal of confusion. As a result, the grieving parents are given *the worst of both worlds*. On the one hand, they still feel the guilt and responsibility that result from their parental failure. But because they are taught and encouraged to deny their responsibility for how their children have turned out, they do not experience the forgiveness that is available to them in Christ. Sin can be forgiven, and the parents can begin the task of interceding for their children, seeking to be used by the Lord in recovering them. But parents who deny responsibility can never experience the relief and joy of forgiveness—as long as they continue to deny what the Bible identifies as sin.

Parental Qualifications for Church Office

Next we should look at the requirements for the elders of the church. This, unfortunately, is a controversial issue. But the fact that it is controversial is not because the Scripture is ambiguous on the point—far from it. It is controversial because these standards reveal the widespread disobedience of the modern evangelical church. We somehow think ourselves wiser than God on what constitutes a qualified pastor or elder. So we will oftentimes say, for example, that a degree from the right seminary is sufficient. God says that a man's household must be managed well—otherwise, how can a man govern in the church? The proving ground for elders is in the home—*not* graduate school.

This whole subject is tragic because it constitutes one of the evangelical church's greatest areas of disobedience. Why do we resist openly homosexual pastors and elders? Because the Scriptures prohibit it. Why do we tolerate pastors with poorly managed homes? The Scriptures prohibit that just as clearly. The answer is that we like to draw the line with *other* people's sins—not our own. But if we were to obey the requirement of Scripture, how many pulpits in our country would be empty next Sunday?

In looking at these requirements, we need to look first at the relationship between the elders of a church and a congregation. The Bible teaches very clearly that elders are not to rule by dictatorial fiat. "Shepherd the flock of God which is among you, serving as overseers, not by compulsion but willingly, not for dishonest gain but eagerly; nor as being lords over those entrusted to you, but being examples to the flock; and when the Chief Shepherd appears, you will receive the crown of glory that does not fade away" (1 Pet. 5:2-4). Peter says that elders are *not* to lord it over those entrusted to them. By contrast, he says that elders are to be *an example*. Now one of the most important areas where the people of God need an effective and biblical example is in the area of child-rearing. If an elder has a home which is a train-wreck, he is *not* being a example to the flock in this crucial area. Given this truth, we should not be surprised that the state of a potential elder's home is expressly stated as part of his qualification for office.

"[An elder must be] one who rules his own house well, having his children in submission with all reverence (for if a man does not know how to rule his own house, how will he take care of the church of God?)" (1 Tim. 3:4-5). The qualification is clear enough. Rule in the home and rule in the church are stated as comparable duties. A poor pastor at home will be a poor pastor in the church. Many might object to this and say that they know of a man who was a tremendous pastor at the church, and yet was a poor father. This is simply an indication of how we have altered the scriptural definition of what constitutes a good pastor in the church. Scripturally, if a man is not qualified to be an elder in the first place, then by definition he is not a good one. Whatever men may say, God speaks differently.

An elder must "rule his own house well." The particular area that Paul singles out here is that of having the children in submission with all reverence. Note that Paul is requiring a father to see to it that his children are *reverently submissive*. It is not sufficient to have children who are bloody and cowed. Paul is not just requiring that the children be externally obedient, he is requiring that they be obedient for the *right reason*, and with the *right attitude*. One reason for this requirement is found a verse later. "Moreover he must have a good testimony among those who are outside, lest he fall into reproach and the snare of the devil" (1 Tim. 3:7). Not only are elders to be an example to the congregation, they are to be a testimony to outsiders. The condition of modern Christianity in our nation can be seen in what has become proverbial among unbelievers on this subject. What is the general reputation of "preacher's kids?" We have this reputation because of *our* disobedience.

Paul says the same thing in Titus when he gives the qualifications for elder there—only in Titus he is, if anything, a little stronger. "[Titus should] set in order the things that are lacking, and appoint elders in every city as I commanded you—if a man is blameless, the husband of one wife, having faithful children not accused of dissipation or insubordination. For a bishop must be blameless, as a steward of God, not self-willed, not quick-tempered, not given to wine, not violent, not greedy for money, but hospitable, a lover of what is good, sober-minded, just, holy, self-controlled, holding fast the faithful word as he has been taught, that he may be able, by sound doctrine, both to exhort and convict those who contradict" (Tit. 1:5-9). There are several interesting things about this passage. An elder must be a "one-woman man." As a result of this union, if he has children, they should be faithful children, children who cannot be accused of riotous living or disobedience. The phrase "faithful children" can also be rendered as "believing children"—in other words, they should be *Christians*, whose lives match their profession. Moreover, the word translated as "riotous living" is *asotia*—literally this means *unsaved*. An elder must not have a rebellious, unsaved child.

But the basic meaning remains unchanged even if we leave the translation as "faithful children." In context, what are they to be faithful *to*? Clearly, they are to be faithful to the teaching and instruction of their father. Now do we want to require children to be faithful when they are told to make their beds or take out the trash, but leave them to their rebellion at the most important point—when they are told to believe on the Lord Jesus Christ? It is hardly possible that Paul is here requiring faithfulness in the little things but indulging faithlessness at the most central area of any Christian parent's concern.

The second interesting thing is that Paul connects this qualification for office to all the others that follow. When he finishes saying what the children of a prospective elder should be like, he then says, "For a bishop must be . . ." In the list that follows, most, if not all, of any disqualifications can be eventually seen in the state of the home. If a man is quick-tempered, for example, who knows all about it? A man who blows up at his children does not necessarily do the same thing in the foyer at church. But the effects of his temper will eventually be seen by the members of the church in the children—unless the church members studiously look the other way, as the Church has been trained to do.

Back in 1 Timothy, Paul gives some qualifications for the office of deacon that are very similar, and which are linked to those for the office of elder. That link is seen in the word *likewise*. "Likewise deacons must be reverent, not double-tongued, not given to much wine, not greedy for money . . . Likewise their wives must be reverent, not slanderers, temperate, faithful in all things. Let deacons be the husbands of one wife, ruling their children and their own houses well" (1 Tim. 3:8, 11-12). Paul tells us that the deacons must be reverent, and that their wives must be reverent. The deacons are to be this way in the same way that the elders are. The elders are to have *reverent children*. The deacons are to be reverent, and to have reverent wives. Both elders and deacons are to rule their own houses well.

It should be clear that God requires responsible and godly family government from all who aspire to any position in church government. Now we should remember that everything the elders do, they do as an *example* to the flock. Christians are expressly told to watch their leaders closely, and imitate them. "Remember those who rule over you, who have spoken the word of God to you, whose faith follow, considering the outcome of their conduct" (Heb. 13:7). Our tragedy of disobedience is that many godly Christian parents are turned away from following the example of their elders. They do this, not because they are rebellious, but because *the elders have not set a biblical example*. Another tragedy is that many Christians *want* a poor example from the elders of the church—it helps them to justify themselves. "Sure, I've had problems with my Bill, but he is no worse than Pastor Smith's kids!"

Now if God requires the leaders of the church to have children who grow up obedient, and in the faith, and if He tells the flock to imitate their godly leaders, what may we conclude? The conclusion is that successful childrearing within the covenant community is a possibility. Not only is it a possibility, *it is required* for those in a position of leadership.

Hard Words/Soft Hearts

We must constantly remember the grace of God. Even when parents have been unfaithful to the covenantal responsibilities given to them, the sovereign mercy of God will sometimes intervene. Consider the tragic contrast between Samuel and Saul. Samuel was a faithful prophet and judge. But as a father, he was disgraced by his sons who took bribes. Saul, on the other hand, was an unfaithful king who had his kingdom taken away because of his unfaithfulness. Nevertheless, he had one of the noblest sons in Scripture—Jonathan.

God remains sovereign in all His dealings. If we are faithful to Him as parents, we are not manipulating Him. He is bound by nothing other than His own Word, freely bestowed and given. He will always do what He has promised.

But what of the parents who have not been faithful and obedient? We must remember that the one who can make sons of Abraham out of rocks can certainly make them out of wayward children as well. Parents who have squandered the opportunity to bring their children up in the Lord will not have that opportunity again. But they may still approach a loving Father with their petitions and requests. Although they have no promises in hand for their children, they may still intercede on behalf of their children. Our God is a God of mercy, and it may please Him to grant the request.

CHAPTER FOUR

Covenant Continuity

Covenant Continuity Between Old and New

We have seen that the promises to parents are constant throughout the Bible. The duties are also constant. But why is this the case? The answer is found in covenantal continuity. The heart of sound biblical parenting is found in an understanding of this *covenantal continuity* between the Old Covenant and the New. This covenantal continuity can be described in this way:

> When we consider God's dealings (actions, commandments, and promises) with His people in the time of the Old Testament, we should believe that His word to them remains in force for us unless He alters the application of it Himself in further revelation.

Modern Christian parents who deny this are cutting themselves off from an immense treasury of promises.

Underlying this is the understanding that the faithful believer in the Old Testament and the faithful under the New Covenant are members together of *one people*. How do we know this is true? As Christians we must turn to Scripture for the answers. The biblical material on this subject is simply immense; a few brief examples will have to suffice.

We see first that the Bible expressly teaches it. Paul says that Israel is the "one olive tree" and compares the transition from Old to New Covenant as one which involved the removal of fruitless branches, and the grafting in of new branches. "For if you were cut out of the olive tree which is wild by nature, and were grafted contrary to nature into a cultivated olive tree, how much more will these, who are natural branches, be grafted into their own olive tree?" (Rom. 11:24). The Gentiles were cut out of a wild olive tree and were grafted into the cultivated olive tree, *which was Israel*. Unbelieving Jews were removed from Israel. The same tree was Israel throughout the process. The Gentiles were warned that the unbelieving Jews were removed because of an unbelieving misunderstanding of the nature of the tree, and that the same thing would happen to them if they fell into unbelief in the same way.

Ethnic Jews are described as the natural branches, and ethnic Gentiles who believe are the branches grafted in. Ethnic Jews who did not believe were cut out. Throughout Paul's discussion, there is only one olive tree, that is, *only one Israel*. Membership in this Renewed Israel is maintained *by faith alone* (11:20). Presumption was the downfall of the Jews and has proven to be the downfall of countless "Christian" Gentiles as well.

In another place, Paul compares Israel under the Levitical administration to a child under age, and the Israel of the New Covenant is that same child grown to his majority. "Now I say that the heir, as long as he is a child, does not differ at all from a slave, though he is master of all, but is under guardians and stewards until the time appointed by the father. Even so we, when we were children, were in bondage under the elements of the world. But when the fullness of the time had come, God sent forth His Son, born of a woman, born under the law, to redeem those who were under the law, that we might receive the adoption as sons" (Gal. 4:1-5). Even though the child Israel has now grown up and matured, he is still the same person. Even though he was indistinguishable from a slave when he was a child, he, the heir, has now grown into his inheritance. Further, it was the good pleasure of the Father to include the believing Gentiles in this inheritance, and to disinherit the unbelieving Jews. Gentiles are now part of the grown heir—the heir that was treated as a slave when he was a child.

In Ephesians, Paul teaches that the previously-excluded Gentiles have now been made citizens of the commonwealth of Israel—"That *at that time* you were without Christ, being aliens from the commonwealth of Israel and strangers from the covenants of promise, having no hope and without God in the world" (Eph. 2:12). There was a time when they were strangers to the covenant promise to Abraham, but they are strangers no longer. The Gentiles have been brought near, they have been brought into Israel. Paul argues here that all ethnic barriers within Israel have come down. He states, "Therefore remember that you, *once Gentiles in the flesh*—who are called Uncircumcision by what is called the Circumcision made in the flesh by hands—that *at that time* you were without Christ, being *aliens from the commonwealth of Israel* and strangers from the covenants of promise, having no hope and without God in the world. But *now* in Christ Jesus you who were once far off *have been made near* by the blood of Christ" (vv. 11-13). It would be difficult to make this any clearer. Gentiles have, through Christ, been made Israelites. They have been brought into the commonwealth of Israel.

Paul does not teach that Israel has been abolished, he teaches that it has been greatly expanded. As James expounded the prophet Amos at the Jerusalem Council, the edges of her tent have been extended to include all nations. "After this I will return and will rebuild the tabernacle of David, which has fallen down; I will rebuild its ruins, and I will set it up; so that the rest of mankind may seek the LORD, even all the Gentiles who are called by My name, says the LORD who does all these things" (Acts 15:16-17). In other words, the calling of the Gentiles is to be understood as rebuilding the ruins of *Israel*, a re-establishment of *David's* tabernacle.

The author of Hebrews teaches that Moses and Christ ministered in the same house—Moses as servant, and Christ as Son.

> And Moses indeed was faithful in all His house as a servant, for a testimony of those things which would be spoken afterward, but Christ as a Son over His own house, whose house we are if we hold fast the confidence and the rejoicing of the hope firm to the end. (Heb. 3:5-6)

In all this we can see that the New Testament emphasizes the continuity between Jewish believers in the Old Testament and believers, both Jew and Gentile, in the New. That continuity is *covenantal* and has a wonderful application to modern covenant families.

Another way we can see this in the New Testament is in the way the apostles apply the law given to the Jews in the Old Testament to the Christian church. For just one of many examples, Paul says,

> For it is written in the law of Moses, 'You shall not muzzle an ox while it treads out the grain.' Is it oxen God is concerned about? Or does He say it altogether for our sakes? *For our sakes, no doubt, this is written*, that he who plows should plow in hope, and he who threshes in hope should be partaker of his hope. (1 Cor. 9:9-10)

Laws passed by Parliament in England are not binding on us here in the United States. So why are laws delivered to the Jews at Sinai binding on modern Americans? The reason is that, according to the New Testament, laws given to them were given to our "fathers"—the New Covenant is made with those whose *fathers* were brought out of Egypt. It is *"not* according to the covenant that I made *with their fathers* in the day when I took them by the hand to lead them out of the land of Egypt" (Heb. 8:9). In the New

Covenant, God writes His laws on the hearts of His people. These people, these New Covenant Christians, must be able to say that God delivered *their fathers* out of the land of Egypt. We are tempted to object, those of us who are Gentiles, because we think our physical fathers were nowhere near Egypt at the time. But the Bible teaches from beginning to end that physical descent considered on its own merit is *worthless*. We are linked with them through God's *covenantal* dealings with Israel, and not by physical ancestry.

The New Covenant was to be made with *Israel*: "I will make a New Covenant with the house of *Israel* and with the house of *Judah*"(Jer. 31:31). At the same time, we see that the New Covenant was made with the *Church*. Paul, an apostle to the Gentiles, was a minister of the New Covenant (2 Cor. 3:6; see also Heb. 8:7-13).

Another important factor in understanding this covenantal continuity is seen in the promises given to the Jews, which are described as fulfilled in the Christian church. For an example concerning the covenantal nature of the believing family, Paul says, "Children, obey your parents in the Lord, for this is right. 'Honor your father and mother,' which is the first commandment *with promise*: 'that it may be well with you and you may live long on the earth'" (Eph. 6:1-3). The book of Ephesians was written to Gentile Christians. In this book, not only does Paul apply a promise contained in the Sinai covenant to *Gentile* Christians, he applies it to Gentile *children*. This was a promise initially given to Jewish *children*—a conditional promise attached to covenantal faithfulness. When it was initially given to Jewish children, it was a covenantal requirement to honor parents that applied to them from their circumcision on. Gentile children, like their parents, used to be strangers to the covenants of promise (Eph. 2:12). But now they are brought near and *included*.

We could look at many more passages than those discussed here. This is only a sample of prophecies and promises given to the Old Israel, which are applied in the New Testament to the New Israel, the Christian church. The New Testament teaches a spiritual and covenantal continuity between the believers under the New Covenant, and the believers under the Old. This is why there is such a clear continuity between parental promises and duties in the Old Testament, and the same promises and duties in the New. And this is why modern Christian parents can receive such great direction and comfort.

The Covenant Nature of Israel

Modern Christians often assume that the Levitical administration of Israel under Moses was a deal God made with ethnic Jews, and that the terms of that covenant were entirely ethnic—*genetic*. The Pharisees believed this and thought the right DNA imprint was sufficient for a right standing with God; modern Christians believe this about those under the Levitical administration and think that it was *insufficient*. But they both believe that this was the way God expected the people in the Old Testament to think. This is false.

In challenging this distortion, the writers of the New Testament do *not* say, "Yes, that is the way it used to be, but there is a new way of doing things now." The biblical writers, in *both* testaments, attack this genetic, ethnic understanding of "Jewishness" with a holy ferocity, labeling it as a fundamental distortion of the *Old* Covenant. Indeed, this misunderstanding of the Old Covenant is one of the reasons a New Covenant was necessary. When God found fault with the people, it was not simply a matter of them disobeying the *terms* of the covenant. Their rebellion was far more serious. It was a case where they distorted the nature of the covenant itself. Consider this warning in the second giving of the Law:

So that there may not be among you man or woman or family or tribe, whose heart turns away today from the LORD our God, to go and serve the gods of these nations, and that there may not be among you a root bearing bitterness or wormwood; and so it may not happen, when he hears the words of this curse, that he blesses himself in his heart, saying, 'I shall have peace, even though I follow the dictates of my heart'— as though the drunkard could be included with the sober. The LORD would not spare him; for then the anger of the LORD and His jealousy would burn against that man, and every curse that is written in this book would settle on him, and the LORD would blot out his name from under heaven. (Deut. 29:18-20)

A man who thought circumcision made him a citizen of Israel, but that he still had a right to live according to his own words, was a fool.

This teaching of the Old Testament was something that was repeated again and again in the New Testament. Paul does not identify the unbelieving Jews as those clinging to an outmoded system; he attacks their theological perversity as something wicked under *all* administrations of the covenant. "Beware of dogs, beware of evil workers, beware of the mutilation!" (Phil. 3:2).

John the Baptist took a dim view of ethnic presumption as well. "And do not think to say to yourselves, 'We have Abraham as our father.' For I say to you that God is able to raise up children to Abraham from these stones" (Mt. 3:9). The apostle John describes this perversion as a form of Satanism. "I know your works, tribulation, and poverty (but you are rich); and I know the blasphemy of those who say they are Jews and are not, but are a synagogue of Satan" (Rev. 2:9). He repeats the same point in the next chapter. "Indeed I will make those of the synagogue of Satan, who say they are Jews and are not, but lie—indeed I will make them come and worship before your feet, and to know that I have loved you" (Rev. 3:9).

We must note what John is claiming here. These synagogues of unbelievers had no right to the title of "Jew." Why? They twisted the covenant God gave them beyond all recognition. They twisted it so far that it was now *satanic*. Had they understood the covenant, they would have believed in Christ.

Although obviously true, it is not enough to say that a Jew cannot be a Christian without Christ. The Bible teaches that a man cannot be a *Jew* without Christ. "For he is not a Jew who is one outwardly, nor is circumcision that which is outward in the flesh; but he is a Jew who is one inwardly; and circumcision is that of the heart, in the Spirit, not in the letter; whose praise is not from men but from God" (Rom. 2:28-29).

Jesus taught the same truth.

> They answered and said to Him, "Abraham is our father." Jesus said to them, "If you were Abraham's children, you would do the works of Abraham. But now you seek to kill Me, a Man who has told you the truth which I heard from God. Abraham did not do this. You do the deeds of your father." Then they said to Him, "We were not born of fornication; we have one Father—God." Jesus said to them, "If God were your Father, you would love Me . . . You are of your father the devil, and the desires of your father you want to do. He was a murderer from the beginning, and does not stand in the truth, because there is no truth in him. When he speaks a lie, he speaks from his own resources, for he is a liar and the father of it. (Jn. 8:39-44)

And Paul, with characteristic bluntness, equates the Judaizing distortion of circumcision with the self-mutilation common among pagans. "And I, brethren, if I still preach circumcision, why do I still suffer persecution? Then the offense of the cross has ceased. I could wish that those who trouble you would even cut themselves off!" (Gal. 5:11-12). The Bible is clear. Ethnicity does not save. Ritual does not save. *Being born into a family which professes faith in God does not save.* Misunderstood, it commonly condemns. When someone trusts in their "tribal position" for salvation, this is a sure indication that they are lost. *Personal individual covenantal faithfulness* is necessary before we may know that God has regenerated and saved any individual. And while it is important to remember this truth, we must also remember that this is *not a new truth.* The truth did not originate in the New Testament at all. God has taught this to parents throughout redemptive history.

Curses in the New Covenant?

One objection to the biblical teaching of covenantal continuity is that the "Old Covenant" was a carnal, external covenant; consequently, the covenant people had to be kept within its bounds with divine threatenings of various *external* kinds. Further, it is argued that in the New Covenant "they will *all* know Me, from the least of them to the greatest," meaning by this that true saving faith is *absolutely universal* in the New Covenant, and that this universal salvation within the covenant is that which distinguishes the Old from the New.

But is the New Covenant in any sense conditional? Can someone fall away from the New Covenant? Does baptism obligate the baptized one to keep the terms of the New Covenant, with *conditional* blessings and curses attached? The unambiguous answer of Scripture to these questions is *yes.* Before proceeding to answer such questions, however, we have to reiterate the scriptural teaching of God's preservation of His saints. No one truly regenerated by the Spirit of God can ever fall away from Christ. Nothing can separate us from the love of God in Christ Jesus. At the same time, the Bible is equally clear that *professing* Christians can and do fall away. When they do, they are not falling from a position of rank unbelief,

they are falling into a covenantal unfaithfulness—just as
so many of the Jews had fallen. Notice how some of these
individuals are described in the book of Hebrews. When a
professing Christian falls away, it is a *covenantal* insult to
the Lord he claimed to serve. "Of how much worse punishment, do you suppose, will he be thought worthy who
has trampled the Son of God underfoot, counted the *blood
of the covenant by which he was sanctified* a common thing,
and insulted the Spirit of grace?" (Heb. 10:29).

The clearest way to see this truth is to study the curses
connected in Scripture to the New Covenant. In 1
Corinthians 10, Paul reminds the Corinthians of the Jews'
baptism into Moses (vv. 1-2) and their subsequent disobedience and chastisement. He then tells these Christians that

> all these things happened to them as examples, and
> they were written for our admonition, upon whom the
> ends of the ages have come. Therefore let him who
> thinks he stands take heed lest he fall. No tempta-
> tion has overtaken you except such as is common to
> man; but God is faithful, who will not allow you to
> be tempted beyond what you are able, but with the
> temptation will also make the way of escape, that you
> may be able to bear it. (1 Cor. 10:11-13)

A central point in this chapter is that the Christians
are not to be faithless to the terms of their baptism into
Christ in the same way the Jews were to their baptism
into Moses. The Jews had a *baptism*, and the Jews had a
covenantal meal in the wilderness, and yet many of them
still fell through unbelief. The Christians at Corinth are
being warned not to fall into the same presumptive sin in
the same way—"*We* have been baptized, and *we* have the
Lord's Supper!" Note the point of Paul's comparison:

> Moreover, brethren, I do not want you to be unaware
> that all our fathers were under the cloud, all passed

through the sea, all were baptized into Moses in the cloud and in the sea, all ate the same spiritual food, and all drank the same spiritual drink. For they drank of that spiritual Rock that followed them, and that Rock was Christ. But with most of them God was not well pleased, for their bodies were scattered in the wilderness. *Now these things became our examples,* to the intent that we should not lust after evil things as they also lusted. (1 Cor. 10:1-6)

We clearly see the presence of curses in the New Covenant. The chastisement that followed Old Testament disobedience is presented as a standing warning to New Covenant believers. *Parents who bring children up in a Christian home must understand these things.* The sin of covenantal presumption remains a standing problem. This presumption is easy because modern Christians often assume that warnings, or cursings, such a prominent feature of the Old Covenant, are absent from the New Covenant— *i.e.* that New Covenant people are not warned in this way. But the Scripture does not bear this out at all.

Jesus warns His disciples in this way. "If anyone does not abide in Me, he is cast out as a branch and is withered; and they gather them and throw them into the fire, and they are burned" (Jn. 15:6). And Paul, when he is comparing the removal of some Jews from Israel, and the inclusion of believing Gentiles, gives those Gentiles a sober warning. "Therefore consider the goodness and severity of God: on those who fell, severity; but toward you, goodness, if you continue in His goodness. Otherwise you also will be cut off . . . For if God did not spare the natural branches, He may not spare you either" (Rom. 11:22, 21; order reversed). The apostle John warns the church at Ephesus in this fashion. "Remember therefore from where you have fallen; repent and do the first works, or else I will come to you quickly and remove your lampstand from its place—unless you repent" (Rev. 2:5).

As discussed above, the apostle Paul warns the Gentile

church at Corinth through a comparison to the behavior
of Israel in the wilderness. The author of Hebrews makes
the same comparison, giving the same kind of warning—

> Therefore, as the Holy Spirit says: 'Today, if you will
> hear His voice, do not harden your hearts as in the re-
> bellion, in the day of trial in the wilderness, where your
> fathers tested Me, tried Me, and saw My works forty
> years. Therefore I was angry with that generation, and
> said, 'They always go astray in their heart, and they
> have not known My ways.' So I swore in My wrath,
> 'They shall not enter My rest.'" Beware, brethren, lest
> there be in any of you an evil heart of unbelief in de-
> parting from the living God; but exhort one another
> daily, while it is called 'Today,' lest any of you be hard-
> ened through the deceitfulness of sin. For we have be-
> come partakers of Christ if we hold the beginning of our
> confidence steadfast to the end, while it is said: 'Today,
> if you will hear His voice, do not harden your hearts as
> in the rebellion'. (Heb. 3:7-15)

The Christians of the first century were being told to stay
far away from an "evil heart of unbelief." If the warning
were neglected, the results would be the same—a harden-
ing through the deceitfulness of sin, followed by the curse
of God.

If the sin is one of *covenantal presumption*, it does not
much matter whether it is Old Covenant presumption or
New Covenant presumption. The judgment of God rests
upon both, and the sin has been a very real one under
both covenants. This is the case because in a believing home,
the promises and duties of the covenant must be taught,
but if they are taught poorly, the temptation will be to
assume that the blessings of the covenant are automatic.
And in a decent home, it is perilously easy to flatter one-
self.

The assumption that cursings are not a feature of the
New Covenant must lead either to the conviction that every

member of any true New Covenant church is necessarily regenerate by definition ("for they will *all* know Me"), or that the New Covenant church is an invisible church known only to God, and that the visible church cannot be described as a New Covenant community (because our observation shows us that, in the visible church, the people do *not* all know God). But scripturally, both options are unacceptable. The first is not the case because the Bible warns us of false brothers within the church, as well as giving the sort of warnings listed above against falling away. The second is not possible because it is the visible church which gathers together to drink the cup of the *New Covenant*. The visible ordinances of the church (baptism and the Lord's Supper) are New Covenant ordinances.

Status of Children in the New Covenant

In what follows, the preceding case for the unity of true Israel—Israel indeed—must be kept constantly in mind. Given the continuity between the Israel of the two covenants, the following biblical statements fit together very naturally. But on the supposition that children of believers are now *outside* the covenant, and have the same covenantal status that a pagan has (or that they somehow float in an undefined third category), the following statements of Scripture do not fit together at all. The application of the following texts is not to children *as such*. Children of disobedient parents are described in Scripture as *unclean*, *children of wrath*, etc. What follows summarizes the Bible's teaching on children in believing homes.

First, we are taught that children of at least one believing parent are *holy*. Another way to translate the word holy is *saint*. In other words, the children of at least one believing parent are saints. "For the unbelieving husband is sanctified by the wife, and the unbelieving wife is sanctified by the husband; otherwise your children would be unclean, but now they are *holy*" (1 Cor. 7:14).

Jesus teaches us that of such children is the kingdom of God. "But Jesus called them to Him and said, "Let the little children come to Me, and do not forbid them; for of such is the kingdom of God (Lk. 18:16). Little children are not removed from the spiritual blessings Christ brings. They are legitimate recipients of *spiritual* blessing. In one of the gospel accounts of this incident, infants—*brephos*—are expressly named. We are taught that children constitute one of the subgroups of the church, to be taught along with the rest of the *saints* in the church. "Paul, an apostle of Jesus Christ by the will of God, To the saints who are in Ephesus, and faithful in Christ Jesus. . . . Children, obey your parents in the Lord, for this is right" (Eph. 1:1; 6:1). The church is assumed to consist of all kinds of people—slaves, parents, husbands, wives, masters, *children*. Paul does the same thing in the book of Colossians. "To the saints and faithful brethren in Christ who are in Colosse: Grace to you and peace from God our Father and the Lord Jesus Christ . . . Children, obey your parents in all things, for this is well pleasing to the Lord" (Col. 1:2; 3:20).

The New Covenant was not brought in to destroy faithful covenantal families. One of its features was to be the restoration of the covenantal father/child relationship, not the dissolution of the covenantal father/child relationship. "He will also go before Him in the spirit and power of Elijah, 'to turn the hearts of the fathers to the children,' and the disobedient to the wisdom of the just, to make ready a people prepared for the Lord" (Lk. 1:17). The New Testament teaches that the responsibility for the reverence and faithfulness of children is delegated to parents. Setting an example to other Christians, a Christian elder must be "one who rules his own house well, having his children in submission with all reverence" (1 Tim. 3:4). We see in the book of Acts that children participated in the devotional exercises of their parents. "When we had come to the end of those days, we departed and went on our way; and they all accompanied us, with wives and children, till we were out of the city. And we knelt down on the shore and prayed" (Acts 21:5).

The Bible teaches that the promised Holy Spirit to Abraham and *his* children is a promise that applies to us and *our* children. "For the promise is to you and to your children, and to all who are afar off, as many as the Lord our God will call" (Acts 2:39). We are taught in the New Testament that conversion involves becoming "as little children." It does not teach that the conversion of little children involves them becoming "as grown-ups." "'Assuredly, I say to you, unless you are converted and become as little children, you will by no means enter the kingdom of heaven'" (Mt. 18:3).

As the growth of the church in the book of Acts indicates, the normal mode of evangelism and baptism in the New Testament was *household by household.* "Now a certain woman named Lydia heard us. She was a seller of purple from the city of Thyatira, who worshiped God. The Lord opened her heart to heed the things spoken by Paul. And when she and her household were baptized, she begged us, saying, 'If you have judged me to be faithful to the Lord, come to my house and stay.' So she persuaded us" (Acts 16:14-15). When the gospel was first promised to Abraham, it was promised as a blessing to all nations. But in one place in the New Testament where this promise is stated, we are taught that the gospel is for the *families* of the earth. "You are sons of the prophets, and of the covenant which God made with our fathers, saying to Abraham, 'And in your seed all the families of the earth shall be blessed'" (Acts 3:25).

CHAPTER FIVE

The Nature of Children and Covenant Nurture

Introduction

A great deal of confusion abounds in the Christian church concerning the nature and status of the children growing up in her midst. In some churches, the children are regarded as little more than short heathens, while in others they are assigned the label *covenant children*, whatever that means. But the Bible clearly teaches us how we are to understand the relationship between the gospel of Christ and the children the Lord has given to us. Parents who neglect this teaching consequently lack both biblical urgency *and* biblical confidence as they undertake the task assigned to them by God. When we learn these truths we may come to teach our children the gospel properly, and be enabled to speak of our children the way the Church speaks of hers in John Newton's wonderful hymn, *Glorious Things of Thee Are Spoken*.

> See, the streams of living waters, springing from
> eternal love,
> Well supply thy sons and daughters and all fear of want
> remove.

The Child By Nature

The Lord tells us in Proverbs 22:15: "Foolishness is bound up in the heart of a child but the rod of correction will drive it far from him." Everyone reading this book is a descendant of Adam, and parents reading this book can see that same sinful reality in their own children. *All of us* were represented by Adam, and were represented *well* by him in his rebellion against God. The individual sins we commit are simply manifestations of our fallen nature which we inherited from our father Adam. In Romans 5 we are told that Death entered the world because one man sinned, and death comes to all men because all sin (Rom. 5:12). Adam was *our* representative and *our* head. Children therefore do not grow up to maturity and *then* decide whether or not they are going to become sinful by nature. Men and women do not come into this world morally neutral. Nor are we born basically good. By nature our entire race is in rebellion against God, and each of us is born into that rebellious race, inheriting the Adamic nature. This reality is not different for Christian homes—it is characteristic of all homes.

Consequently, the only thing each child lacks in order to begin sinning is intelligence and the requisite muscle strength. Every child is self-centered by nature, and thus simply grows and is amplified over time. Parents do not have to go into the play room in order to teach children how to grab toys from one another or to scream "Me! me! me!" All of us, *by nature*, are objects of God's wrath. This means that every child, apart from the intervening grace of God, is under the wrath of God. This is a truth we must learn from Scripture, and not through a fond perusal of the child's baby book. We need to realize that every moral monster our race has ever produced (and there have been many) was once a cute baby. We cannot draw our assessment of human nature from outward appearances. Man looks on the outward appearance, and God looks on the heart (1 Sam. 16:7). Given the opportunity, sin will *always* manifest itself in our children.

Parental instruction and discipline are necessary to restrain that sin, and deal with it effectively. But the purpose of parental discipline is not to keep sin from appearing. Many Christian parents are appalled at the first lie or malevolent action they see in their children, and they assume that the problem must have originated with their child's new playmates down the street. But the problem comes from the child's heart—Christ teaches us that sin proceeds from the heart. We must therefore always remember that discipline is not a substitute for the gospel. Properly understood and applied, godly discipline is a God-ordained preparation for a right understanding of the gospel.

But many Christian parents fall into a humanistic understanding of sin. When their child begins to manifest this *inbred and natural sin*, they blame that little pagan neighbor kid. Or "our child" must be picking it up from some bad companions somewhere else. Now a boy down the street may be able to teach new techniques or new words, but the *desire* to be sinful comes from Adam and *not* from our surrounding environment. So every child who comes into the home is therefore by nature a little bundle of unfocused sin. It is simply a matter of time before this child's sin is manifested in the home.

Eternal consequences are connected to this. Sin always has consequences, and not just for the present. Proverbs 23:13-14 says: "Do not withhold correction from a child, for if you beat him with a rod, he will not die. You shall beat him with a rod, *and deliver his soul from hell.*" Children are eternal beings. They are going to live forever *somewhere*, either in union with God or separated from Him. Because they are creatures who will live eternally, the way in which they are shaped in their upbringing has eternal consequences. How the parents treat them, or refuse to treat them, affects that eternal destination.

Unfortunately, the Bible contains many examples of parents who did not do what God required, and the poor job of childrearing resulted in wrecked lives. One such instance is found in 1 Kings 1:5-6: "Now Adonijah the

son of Haggith exalted himself, saying, 'I will be king';
. . . (And *his father had not rebuked him at any time* by
saying, 'Why have you done so?')" Adonijah wanted to be
king. But why? His father David had failed him; he had
not said *no* to his son at any time. Adonijah eventually lost
his life because of David's negligence. We see this same
sort of indulgence with Absalom. After David's death,
Solomon, David's successor, had to put Adonijah to death
because he was still scheming for the throne. David will
be in heaven; he was a man after God's own heart. But he
was not the kind of father he should have been, and some
of his children will not be there with him.

Another example of this can be found in 1 Samuel
3:11-13. The Lord came to the young boy Samuel and gave
him a message. Samuel had grown up under Eli at the tabernacle of the Lord. "Then the Lord said to Samuel:
'Behold, I will do something in Israel at which both ears
of everyone that hears it will tingle. In that day I will perform against Eli all that I have spoken concerning his house,
from beginning to end. For I have told him that I will
judge his house forever for the iniquity which he knows,
because his sons made themselves vile, *and he did not restrain them.*'" Eli was an old man at this time. His sons
were grown men, but he was still held responsible for not
having restrained them. Both Eli's sons came to an inglo-
rious end because their father did not say *no* to them.

God brought death to the sons of both David and Eli.
In the Scriptures there are men of God who will be in
heaven, but whose sons will not be. Eli was an indulgent
father and his sons were destroyed. Samuel *himself*, the
one who had come to Eli and rebuked Eli for what had
happened, had sons who grew up and took bribes. This
Samuel was later used by God to rebuke Saul, who was a
disobedient man. But Samuel's sons did not turn out, while
Saul's sons, Jonathan and Ishbosheth, are among the nobles.

We all know parents who really are among God's people,
but in the area of parenting they failed miserably, and their

children suffer the consequences. Some Christian parents do not want to obey God in the area of child-rearing. They look at families which take child rearing responsibilities very seriously, and say, *"Just wait* till your child is in the terrible two's. *Then* you will be sorry you took this hard line." Or they will utter warnings like: *"Just wait* until they are in school," or "Wait until he is a *teenager."* And then when the children of obedient parents grow up to walk with the Lord, carping observers say, "Oh, that's very well for you to say, you've got good kids." *But good children are not an accident.* God gives *everyone* rotten children.

The Child In Covenant

If we only consider what we are *by nature*, the prospects can be pretty discouraging. But as we saw in Chapter 2, God has given us some great and precious promises concerning our children. We have considered what our children are by nature, but this is not everything the Bible teaches on the subject. We must remember what our children are *by covenant*. The apostle Paul tells us that there is a distinction to be made between the children of believers and the children of unbelievers. "For the unbelieving husband is sanctified by the wife, and the unbelieving wife is sanctified by the husband; otherwise your children would be unclean, but now they are holy" (1 Cor. 7:14). Two kinds of children are presented to us. The children of unbelievers are called *unclean.* The word used is *akathartos* and means *foul* or *unclean.* The word is used most frequently to describe unclean demonic spirits. The children of believers are called *holy.* The word used is *hagia* and is commonly rendered as *saint.* The Bible gives us a clear distinction between the children of at least one believer and the children of unbelievers. But is that distinction personal and individual? Is it to be found *in* the children?

We have already established that our children are by

nature indistinguishable from all other human children. Paul is not teaching us here that our newborn infants are all regenerate and personally holy. He is teaching us *their covenantal status*. They are holy by virtue of their placement in a covenanted family. If they were outside the covenant, they would be unclean. Because they are not, they are set apart as holy.

Because we cannot talk to infants in order to find out their thoughts and convictions, we do not know what their actual status is. Some of them may indeed be regenerate. John the Baptist was filled with the Spirit from the womb (Lk. 1:15). Christ spoke of those children who were able to praise God from their mothers' breasts (Mt. 21:16). At the same time, because we cannot see the heart, it is impossible for us to *assume* anything about an infant's personal standing before God. Nevertheless, we may believe God's Word when He tells us that our children have been set apart for Him. We must therefore hold to this covenantal promise until we see clear *scriptural* evidence to the contrary. The wonderful thing is, if we hold to the covenantal promise scripturally, we will not find scriptural evidence to the contrary.

A grown man who professes faith in Christ and is baptized has come into a covenantal relationship with God. Is this man *genuinely* converted? God knows and has told us that we are to judge such matters (tentatively, in the manner of creatures) on the basis of visible fruit. In the same way, a child, set apart as holy from birth, should be treated as a partaker of the covenantal blessings of Christ. As the child grows, he *will* exhibit the fruit of his nature— regenerate or otherwise. Some covenant children are regenerate and some are not. How do we tell the difference? We make such determinations on the basis of *profession* and *fruit*. Wise parents will therefore not assume that their child is automatically regenerate. *Neither will they assume the opposite*. They will evaluate their child's life and profession in the light of Scripture. But it is important to note here that a wise evaluation will not assume that a child is unregenerate simply because he sins. What would happen if *we* were evaluated according to the standard we sometimes apply to our children? The Bible teaches us that assurance of salvation is not found in sinlessness, but rather in our attitude toward our sin and the conviction of the Holy Spirit. Are we responsive to the forgiveness offered in Christ?

The Child In Grace

But godly parents will want to know more than the fact their children are set apart covenantally at birth. The one who perseveres to the end will be saved. The one who is faithful throughout life is the one who has made his calling and election sure. While God has set apart His elect from before the foundation of the world, we can only see election through the fruit of it. True covenant children can and do fall away. Birth into a covenant home is by no means an *automatic* ticket to heaven. For this reason, godly parents want to see their children grow up to a faithful and consistent profession. Such a consistent profession is impossible apart from the regenerative grace of God.

In some cases, faithful parents will find themselves leading a child *in grace*. With other children, they may be used to lead them *into grace*. The assurance of parents, and then later, the assurance of the child, should not be based upon a distinct conversion event in the life of the child. A man does not need to know what time the sun rose in the morning in order to know that it is up. In a similar way, the father and mother do not need to tell exactly when the sun rose in their child's life in order to see the evidences of grace. The fruit of the Spirit is as obvious as sunshine. If love, joy, and peace are in that child's life and they have grown up in it, they may not be able to pinpoint the day or the hour they were born again. This may be frustrating to some, but we should remember that those brought up apart from Christ commonly wish that they had had a biblical upbringing. Assurance of salvation for the child rests upon the same ground as it does with any other believer—and this is not the assurance that comes from a human action or decision. Assurance comes from believing Christ, and gratefully noting the promised results of believing Christ.

This kind of biblical upbringing provides an important barrier God places between the child and eternal destruction. We all know people who were brought up in some horrible way, and we rejoice how God redeemed them regardless. But the evangelical world has placed too great a value on the "flashy testimony." God teaches us, in His ordinary providence, that parents are to bring their children up in godliness, with those children never having known anything else.

If a garden is left untended, it will be full of weeds and will not *normally* produce fruit. If a child is left alone and then is brought back from the edge of the pit through conversion, it will be because of an extraordinary intervention by God and His extension of grace. However, God has designed the institution of the family to work in a very ordinary way. But many Christian parents hang everything on a big roll of the dice. They say, "Our child is at college, and I just hope and pray that God brings some Christian into his life. . . ." They are hoping for some remarkable divine intervention after eighteen years of negligence on their part. In such a case, God might intervene and He might not. But if parents obey in how they bring the children up, those children will walk with God the rest of their lives. As we saw earlier, the familial qualifications for an elder in the church are clear. Now if an elder is required not to be a violent man, then we presume that he has control over whether or not he is a violent man. If the requirement is that the elder not be given over to much wine, then he has control over that. He cannot say these things are outside of his control. In the same way, he must have believing children. Many modern evangelical pastors speak as if they have no control over this. They advise just taking the children to church and hoping for the best. This crapshoot approach to child-rearing is *dead wrong*.

Under the promised grace of God, fathers *can* control whether or not their children grow up to walk with God. Are their children going to spend eternity in heaven because of how they were loved, spanked, read to, and prayed with? Or are they going to be saved, if they are saved, in spite of their parents? Godly parents should want to be the instrument that God has given to their children through whom they will be saved. The message of salvation will not be normally heard apart from discipline. Discipline or law is not the gospel, but the gospel does not make any sense apart from the law.

Discipline is an artificially negative consequence. When a child becomes old enough to get really destructive, leave home, and wreck his life, the consequences are real and forever. When a toddler is spanked, the consequences are momentary—and in a certain sense *unreal*—but he is being taught to associate sin and punishment. When the child is older, he has already learned that when he sins, something very destructive happens. This understanding of law is preparation for understanding the gospel.

Yeah, But . . .

Some Christians may object to all this as undercutting a proper understanding of the sovereignty of God's election. The Bible teaches that election is unconditional. That is, before the foundation of the world, God chose those who were to be saved, and He did so without regard to any merit or choices on their part. But if we argue (as we have been) that the behavior of parents affects or *conditions* how their children turn out, then how can we still say that election is unconditional? Doesn't this make salvation of some (the children) dependent upon the faith *and works* of others (the parents)? And how is this consistent with the sovereignty of grace?

The answer to this question depends upon a distinction long maintained among historic Protestant theologians. When we say that we are saved by grace through faith, we do not maintain that our faith is the ground of our justification. If it were the ground of our justification, then we would be saved *because of* something we do, and those who are not saved would not be saved *because of* something they did not do. This obviously undercuts the Bible's teaching on salvation by grace. Consequently, classical Protestant theology has long maintained the distinction between faith as the *instrument* of our justification and the efficacious death of Christ as the *ground* of our justification. And even the instrument of our salvation must be considered a gift from God, so that no one can even be tempted to boast (Eph. 2:8-10). This distinction acknowledges the complete sovereignty of God over our salvation, and at the same time recognizes that the sovereign God uses human instruments to accomplish His purposes.

So our faith is the *instrument* of our justification. But prior to repentance and belief we also see *lesser instruments* in the hand of God as well. In the area of salvation, the sovereign God has determined to use *means* in order to implement His sovereign pleasure. In bringing sinners into a relationship with Him, one of those means is the proclamation of the gospel. Apart from this providentially ordained *means*, which is the appointed task of the church, there is no ordinary hope of salvation. The Westminster Confession of Faith puts it this way:

> The visible church . . . consists of all those throughout the world that profess the true religion, together with their children; and is the kingdom of the Lord Jesus Christ, the house and family of God, out of which there is no ordinary possibility of salvation. (XXV/2)

The work and ordinances of the visible church are the *means* God uses to implement His will for the salvation of the elect.

These distinctions are well understood in classical Protestant circles when the subject concerns how adults are brought to salvation. Why does the same distinction become difficult when we are dealing with the salvation of our children? If a preacher does not go and preach to the sinner, then he will not hear. If he does not hear, how can he believe? If he does not believe, how can he be saved?

> For "whoever calls on the name of the LORD shall be saved." How then shall they call on Him in whom they have not believed? And how shall they believe in Him of whom they have not heard? And how shall they hear without a preacher? And how shall they preach unless they are sent? As it is written: "How beautiful are the feet of those who preach the gospel of peace, Who bring glad tidings of good things!" (Rom. 10:13-15)

If a preacher is necessary for the salvation of sinners (and he ordinarily is), then does this make the preaching of grace a *work*? As Paul might say, "May it never be!" God gives the preacher as one small part of His *gift*. God *sends* the preacher. The preaching of the gospel is an ordained means of bringing sinners to Christ.

Moreover, this does not just apply to the *fact* of preaching—it applies to the *manner* of presentation as well. If a preacher does not go, then sinners will not believe. If the preacher speaks without authority (as the scribes), or harshly, or incompetently, then in the ordinary providence of God, the results will be poor. If he preaches in the power of God, the way God requires, the results will be different. "Now it happened in Iconium that they went together to the synagogue of the Jews, *and so spoke* that a great multitude both of the Jews and of the Greeks believed" (Acts 14:1). The way they preached, under the sovereignty of God, was important. The messenger of the cross should not be obnoxious. "And a servant of the Lord must not quarrel but be *gentle* to all, able to teach, *patient*, in *humility* correcting those who are in opposition, *if* God perhaps will grant them repentance, so that they may know the truth . . ." (2 Tim. 2:24-25). The *manner* of the messenger is connected to the *possibility* (from our vantage point) of the sovereign God giving the wonderful gift of repentance.

The sovereign God gives and sends parents as well. He *gives* parents to children. When He has ordained eternal life for these children, His ordinary pattern described in Scripture is to give them godly parents. The parents are *not* the ground of their children's salvation; godly parents most emphatically *are* an ordained instrument of it. Christian parents are often tempted to shrink from this responsibility, and sometimes a "doctrinal objection" provides the necessary cover. But we must always guard our hearts. We received our children from God—do we dare reject His words which came with this gift? We want to cry out, with Paul, "Who is sufficient for these things?" (2 Cor. 2:16). We must come to the same answer Paul did—our sufficiency is from God (2 Cor. 3:5).

At the same time, two central differences exist between preachers to the lost and "preachers to covenant children." Ordinary preachers have normally been given no promises concerning the responsiveness of particular hearers. Perhaps God will give repentance, perhaps not. The godly preacher must be humble and pray that God will be merciful. But godly parents have been given *promises*. The second distinction is that preachers of the gospel are not required to focus their labors with a set group of individuals. Parents, on the other hand, know the precise boundaries of their field of ministry. Because God has given promises to parents who follow His Word, we may distinguish the evangelism of a pagan neighbor from the process of bringing our little ones to understand and embrace the grace of God in Christ. Instead of using the word "evangelism," I call the latter process *covenant nurture*.

Another possible objection comes from the record of biblical parents. What about Jacob and Esau, for example? Two answers come to mind, both applicable. First, the sovereign God is free to make exceptions. This is something we understand well in other areas—one does not usually follow the "Hosea pattern" for finding a wife. Few Christians take Abraham's sacrifice of Isaac as a normative pattern for today. In the same way, if God wanted to teach the sovereignty of election through giving an Esau to obedient parents, He is the Lord. It would be foolish for us to resist Him at that point, and *equally* foolish to set aside His promises to parents on the basis of such actions. He is the Lord and may do what He wills and promise what He wills. As creatures our responsibility is to submit to His works and *His words*.

Having established this principle, we may still say that we have no examples from Scripture of parents who submitted to the will of God *for their children*, only to see their children fall away from the grace of God. Isaac provides a good example of this. When Rebekah was still pregnant, God had revealed that the older would serve the younger (Gen.25:23), and yet Isaac still favored Esau (Gen.25:28). Isaac fully intended to bless Esau contrary to God's expressed will (Gen. 27:29). In Isaac's misapplied blessing, he intended for Jacob to serve Esau. This is not said to excuse Jacob's deception, but rather to point out Isaac's disobedience with regard to his children. We would have to look elsewhere for an example in Scripture of God giving a reprobate child to parents faithful to their covenantal responsibilities *as parents*.

Covenant Instruction

This is a subject which is too commonly neglected in Christian teaching on bringing up children. It is the part of our duty which, unfortunately, many do not consider a duty at all. Many parents *expect too little*. One of the curses of modern child-rearing is the low ethical and intellectual standard we set for our children. This was not always the case. Consider this excerpt of a letter from Isaac Watts, Sr. to his children, the *oldest* of whom was eleven.

> Though I cannot speak to you, yet I pray for you; and do hope that my God will hear me, and in due time bring me to live again amongst you, if he shall see such a mercy fit to be bestowed on me or you. However, we must endeavor by patient waiting to submit to his will without murmuring; and not to think amiss of his chastening us, knowing that all his works are the products of his infinite wisdom, his designs are the advancement of his own glory; and his ends towards his people their sanctification and salvation, which certainly shall be accomplished at last, however his great providences may seem contrary to it, as to our apprehensions. . . .

We also see this expectation in Scripture. In Deuteronomy 6, there was no instruction to "dumb down" the instruction in the law.

Parents must resist the temptation to *treat children as non-spiritual beings*. Children bear the image of God, and they will show a natural interest in spiritual things, and they will respond to the light of truth in the same way others do. Although they live in immaturity, this simply means there will be an immature rebellion against the light, or an immature believing response to it. Children do not receive a soul later on in life. Related to this, parents should avoid *treating children as autonomous beings*. God did not design them to live in this way, and parents should not treat them as though He did. In other words, suppose the father is explaining to the children the doctrinal differences between their church and the church attended by some of their friends at school. The father should not be embarrassed by the question, "What do *we* believe?"

Children trust the teaching authority of their parents because God designed them that way. The commands in Scripture we have already considered presuppose this.

Moralism is especially dangerous. The teaching children receive from Scripture should be biblically balanced. There is a great temptation to emphasize ethical behavior in child-rearing, to the neglect of doctrinal instruction. This readily downgrades into moralism, Pharisaism, *etc.* But the only way to guard against self-righteousness in a moral home is by teaching *doctrine*: justification, grace, imputation, *etc.* There is no good reason for teaching the children the last three chapters of Ephesians while neglecting the first three.

Another trap to avoid is that of *getting into sin while teaching.* When teaching children, a parent must discipline and teach simultaneously. If a child is getting on dad's nerves while he is in the middle of a sentence about the great mercies of Christ, the resultant problems should be apparent.

It should be obvious, but the first duty of Christian parents is to bring children in contact with the biblical data. This is done through reading the Bible, reading Bible stories, listening to Bible tapes, *etc.* In the second place, this is done through the reading of godly and instructive books. This includes books like *The Chronicles of Narnia*, biographies of missionaries, *etc.* In our home, the best place for godly instruction has been, not surprisingly, *dinner table discussion.* This is a very practical application of the instruction of Deuteronomy 6. Parents can teach vocabulary and doctrine at the same time. They can take advantage of questions. They can integrate the Word of God with what is going on around them or out in the world. For example, I don't know how many times my children have been watching news with me, and then asked me about a certain report, "Is that bad?" And when parents answer such questions, it must be based on the *Word*.

Another important aspect of teaching the Word is a

time of formal instruction. There are many good books and catechisms available. At the same time, it is important not to catechize the children in such a way as to make them disgusted with such rote learning for life. Parents must *give the sense*, and give it in an atmosphere of warmth and love.

Assurance of Salvation

The most efficient means of filling up a good church with unregenerate people is for parents who are church members to neglect their children. Consequently, it is important that parents diligently pray and work toward the child's profession of faith, watching carefully for the attendant fruit of true regeneration. When a child has come to a profession of faith, it should be measured against the same standard as everyone else's profession. A man's salvation is Christ; a child's salvation is also Christ. In both cases, they must look to Christ for assurance.

"Examine yourselves as to whether you are in the faith. Test yourselves. Do you not know yourselves, that Jesus Christ is in you?—unless indeed you are disqualified" (2 Cor. 13:5). Parents must also remember Peter's words. "Therefore, brethren, be even more diligent to make your calling and election sure, for if you do these things you will never stumble . . ." (2 Pet. 1:10). The basic elements necessary in order to bring children to faith are plain. A sinner (in this case the child), a presenter of the gospel (the parent), the law of God, and the gospel of Christ must all be present. When parents are teaching their children the only way of salvation, *they must not modify* the content of law or the gospel.

Parents must not try to talk the children into becoming Christians. If care is not taken, they will be inoculated to true Christianity. Such inoculation occurs when someone gets a small enough amount to protect him against the real thing. Remember, parents are not recruiters. They should not turn their kids into *decisionists*. No one is a Christian *because* he prayed a prayer at a particular time.

Christian parents must not teach, and must not let their children assume, that a genuine profession of faith is unnecessary. Multitudes of "decent" folks have grown up under the hearing of the gospel and have assumed that, of course, conversion is not necessary for *them*. This mistake, with horrific eternal consequences, is a mistake which occurs in churches all the time. So those things which the father and mother *believe* about the gospel are important. Salvation is in the sovereign hand of God, and the contents of the Book of Life are none of our business (Deut. 29:29). We are not the librarian or keeper of that Book. Now many children of believing parents do not become believers themselves. At the same time, children of obedient believers *will become believers*. "Train up a child in the way he should go, and when he is old he will not depart from it" (Prov. 22:6). The sovereign God uses means to accomplish His purposes in election, and His appointed and revealed means for the conversion of covenant children is obedient parents—not elect parents who are disobedient in how they bring up children.

Children who are unregenerate will come to this awareness *on their own*. They will know they are in need of salvation. Parents should pray that God would enable them to distinguish normal child-like openness and the time when they are genuinely spiritually tender. Parents should not cater to their child's autonomy; they should seek assurance that the Holy Spirit is at work. The time of openness should not be "brought about" through some parental manipulation. As the parents trust God and avoid evangelistic manipulation, God will bless.

As children grow up in a faithful covenant home, they will come to a genuine profession of faith as a matter of course. Consequently, parents must teach them, pray for them, maintain fellowship with them, and bring them up to maturity in Christ.

CHAPTER SIX

The Authority of Parents

As parents labor in the great work of childrearing, it is important that they remember who they are. God has invested parents with a very great authority, and this authority must be taken very seriously by parents. Unless parents take this authority seriously, the children certainly will not.

Exodus 21:17 states: "And he who curses his father or his mother shall surely be put to death." To curse father or mother was a capital crime in ancient Israel. If a child said "God damn you," or "Go to hell," his life was forfeit. Now many Christians today support the death penalty for serial murderers because the Bible says that capital punishment is required in certain cases. And even many non-Christians agree that axe murderers should be executed. But these same Christians can become troubled when they read through the Old Testament—because, to continue our example, cursing father or mother also carried the death penalty.

But the problem grows. If we turn to the New Testament, our embarrassment is not relieved. In Mark 7:5-13, our Savior confronts the Pharisees and Scribes:

> Then the Pharisees and Scribes asked Him, "Why do your disciples not walk according to the tradition of the elders, but eat bread with unwashed hands?" He answered and said to them, "Well did Isaiah prophesy of

you hypocrites, as it is written, 'This people honors Me
with their lips but their heart is far from Me and in vain
they worship Me, teaching as doctrines the commandments of men.' For laying aside the commandment of
God, you hold the tradition of men, the washing of
pitchers and cups and many other such things you do."
And He said to them, "All too well you reject the commandment of God, that you may keep your tradition.
For Moses said, 'Honor your father and your mother
and he who curses father or mother, let him be put to
death.' But you say, 'If a man says to his father or
mother, "Whatever profit you might have received from
me is corban"'(that is a free gift from God), then you
no longer let him do anything for his father or mother,
making the word of God of no effect through your tradition which you have handed down. And many such
things you do."

Jesus uses, without embarrassment, a portion of the
Old Testament which atheists and agnostics gleefully use
in letters to the editor in order to humiliate modern Christians. "You can't appeal to the *Bible*! Why, the Bible requires the death penalty for words spoken in the heat of a
domestic spat!" But we should note what is happening in
this portion of Mark. Jesus was confronting the religious
leaders of His day because they had *set aside the Word of
God* for the sake of traditions of *men*. Our Lord acknowledges that not honoring father or mother is a capital crime,
and death is an appropriate punishment for the guilty. He
has no problem with this. On the contrary, He has a problem
with setting the requirement aside.

To curse father or mother, whether by physical attack or through verbal cursing, is a horrible evil and is
deserving of punishment by death. As with *all* sin, forgiveness is available in the sacrifice of Christ. But we must
never seek to magnify forgiveness by minimizing the sin.
We need to recapture the biblical perspective of how grievous
sin is, and in particular how grievous *this* sin is. Jesus quotes

this passage showing that God requires that parents be honored, and He also shows that obedience to this is not a trifle.

In Exodus 21, God invests parents with *His* authority, and applies the sanctions of His law to protect that authority. We honor our father and mother, not because *they* say to do so, but in obedience to *God*. Many Christians parents are good parents, and they exercise their authority in a responsible way. But godly parents are not the ones who have a problem with their children cursing them. In this passage, the authority of God is applied to parents who are *failures*. The parents in question have brought up a child *who has turned on them and cursed them*. As we have already seen, if the child has been brought up correctly, it would not have happened. God does not give the law with built-in hedges—"He who curses his father or mother, provided said father or mother did everything right in the process of child-rearing, shall be put to death." Such a qualification would be superfluous. If the father and mother had done what they were supposed to do, the incident would not have happened. If a child is brought up in the way he should go, he will not depart from it in the end. So the requirement here means that the law of God requires that *poor* parents must be honored. The parents here did not bring up their child under God's promises (obviously), and yet God still requires the execution of the cursing child. This means that, biblically speaking, children cannot use the failure of parents as an excuse for their own sin. *Parental failure is not a defense.*

In our society, the tendency is to justify the sin of the children by pointing out the sins, real and imagined, of the parents. Counselees by the carload are discovering that they were "abused" as children. Without minimizing the horrible problem with those who really *were* abused—physically assaulted, tortured, killed, pushed out of windows, used in pornographic movies—it is necessary to protest, in the strongest possible way, our rampant "abuse" inflation. We must never forget that the humanistic definition of "abuse" includes godly discipline.

For example, in Numbers 12:11-14, we read this account of Moses interceding for his sister: "Aaron said to Moses, 'Oh my lord, please do not lay this sin on us in which we have done foolishly and in which we have sinned. Please do not let her be as one dead, whose flesh is half consumed when he comes out of his mother's womb.' So Moses cried out to the Lord, saying, 'Please heal her, O God, I pray.' Then the Lord said to Moses, 'If her father had but spit in her face, would she not be shamed seven days? Let her be shut out of the camp seven days, and after that she may be received again.'"

Completely apart from the narrative concerning Miriam, we learn something else in passing. In the camp of the Israelites, what would happen if a father spit in his daughter's face? The daughter was excluded from the camp for seven days; the *daughter* was in disgrace. Now it should be obvious that any father who resorts to that kind of treatment of his daughter is a father who has *not* done what God requires of him. But even though this is so, God's authority still rests with the *parents*. This passage depicts a man who is driven by the behavior of his daughter to react in a way that disgraces his daughter. When that happens, the daughter is the one who is left outside the camp, not the father. Today, we would lock the father up, and justify ourselves by saying that he is clearly a failure as a parent. This is quite true—*he is*. But again, even though the parents are failures, the authority of God still rests upon them.

Ephesians 6:1-3 states: "Children, obey your parents in the Lord, for this is right. Honor your father and mother, which is the first commandment with a promise, that it may be well with you and you may live long on the earth." In order to gain the honor due them from their children, the parents must first honor *their* own parents. Many Christians who are struggling as parents are doing so because they are still disobedient to God *as children*. We must remember that whether or not our parents have been ungodly, or failures, *has nothing to do with the command given to us*. We are to honor our parents for no other reason than that God saw fit to make them our parents. Our children will not have a great example if we refuse to do what God requires of us for *our* parents.

Many adults will defend their dishonoring of their parents by saying that their parents are not respectable. But God does not require us to honor them because they are respectable. He says that we are to honor them because they are our father and mother.

For many Christians parents, a restitution letter to *their* parents is necessary and is the first step in the proper rearing of their own children. When a child sends a restitution letter, the point is to confess years of not honoring parents. The point of letter-writing is simple. This is the best method in families where communication has broken down, and where conversations very quickly deteriorate into quarrels. In writing a letter of apology and respect, it does not matter if the parent is "a sinner." We are all sinners. He must be honored anyway. And even though he is a sinner, it is quite possible that a resentful child has been blinded by bitterness and cannot see many admirable qualities in the parent. If a poor parent gets right with God, he is going to have to repent of what was done to the family. But this does not set aside the obligation of the child; the child's business is to obey God and honor his parents.

If an adult child does not honor his parents, his authority with his own children will be built on sand. Many of the problems we have with our children can be traced to the disrespect and dishonor that we have toward our parents.

Some might say that to emphasize parental authority is to destroy friendship between parents and children. Now it does destroy peer friendship. The father and mother are not their child's peers, *and they should not want to be.*

God has given them a unique relationship to their children so the children should always look up to their parents with respect. The parent is in authority over the child. The child can never pass his parents up. Having said this, biblical authority does *not* destroy family intimacy. There can be true intimacy within the framework of a such authority. After all, true Christians cry *Abba* through the Spirit. We are taught to pray to our Father, but in the next breath we are to hallow His name. So we must never say that for the sake of intimacy we must allow disrespect of the father or mother's position.

The Christian parent is God's appointed representative to the child to speak and apply God's Word. We are to address our children in this way, clearly stating what we expect of them, and showing them how this expectation of ours is God's expectation for them. We are to teach those portions of Scripture which make this point, and we are to teach them from these passages in such a way as to make the sense clear.

CHAPTER SEVEN

The Necessity of Christian Education

Is a Christian education something which Christian parents are morally obligated to provide for their children? In order to argue in the affirmative, we must seek to place the ground of the obligation in the plain reading of Scripture. If a prohibition or requirement is not based on Scripture, no true moral obligation is involved.

As Christians, we must begin with the assumption that there is no area of life where biblical principles are irrelevant. So even though the Bible does not directly address every problem in the modern world *with our terminology* (including the problems posed by the existence of government education), nevertheless, the Scriptures do address the problem in a very clear way. God *has* revealed in His Word how He wants us to rear and educate our children.

In saying this, it is important to distinguish things which differ. Nowhere does the Bible label as sin the practice called "sending a child to government school." Consequently, we must imitate the Scriptures in this. At the same time, the Bible is very clear on the central parental responsibility in education, and this *principle*, when applied to our contemporary situation, provides us with clear direction.

To guard against misunderstanding, we should begin with a definition of "government schools." For the purposes of our discussion in this chapter, a government school is an officially agnostic, tax-supported institution of education for dependent children. Frankly, quite aside from the following arguments, I believe any Christian who grants this definition must immediately concede that a strong case has already been made. And anyone who denies the definition will have trouble maintaining his case because the definition is so obviously descriptive of what we call the government or public schools here in America. Having given this definition, we may turn to the scriptural arguments for the necessity of Christian education.

First, Christian parents are morally obligated to keep their children out of government schools because the Scriptures expressly require a non-agnostic form of education. Consider this passage in Deuteronomy on the instruction of children. "Hear, O Israel: The Lord our God, the Lord is one! You shall love the Lord your God with all your heart, with all your soul, and with all your might. And these words which I command you today shall be in your heart; you shall teach them diligently to your children, and shall talk of them when you sit in your house, when you walk by the way, when you lie down, and when you rise up. You shall bind them as a sign on your hand, and they shall be as frontlets between your eyes. You shall write them on the doorposts of your house and on your gates" (Deut. 6:4-9). We should remember that this required instruction in the law of God was not limited to "spiritual truths." It involved agriculture, economics, history, sex education, *etc.*—what we call education today. The biblical mind is not compartmentalized into two distinct areas of thought: secular and sacred. All of life is under the authority of God's revealed Word, and children were to be taught in terms of this comprehensive authority *all the time*.

The same mentality about the instruction of children can be seen in the New Testament: "Children, obey your parents in the Lord, for this is right. 'Honor your father and mother,' which is the first commandment with a promise: 'that it may be well with you and you may live long on the earth.' And you, fathers, do not provoke your children to wrath, but bring them up in the training and admonition of the Lord" (Eph. 6:1-4). The word translated *training* in verse four is *paideia*. This word refers to the "whole training and education of children." The responsibility for seeing that this happens rests with the child's father, and he is required to see to it that the entire educational process is "of the Lord."

In the Deuteronomy passage the requirement is that children live in an environment pervaded by Scripture. A thorough and biblical instruction can only be provided successfully if it is happening *all the time*. Teaching in terms of God's law must occur when walking, driving, sitting, and when lying down. Nothing could be clearer—God wants the children of His people to *live* in an environment conditioned by His Word. In Ephesians, we see the same thing, and it is stated just as directly. Children are to be brought up *in* something; that something is the Word of God. The arrival of the New Covenant did not make godly education somehow optional. We can consider the question another way. What area of life has God declared to be neutral, in which it is permissible to ignore Him, and His Word, while we instruct our children? The answer is that there is no such neutral zone; it does not exist.

Secondly, Christian parents are morally obligated to keep their children out of the public schools because of the requirements involved in keeping the greatest commandment. Jesus requires His people to love the Lord their God with all their *minds* (Mt. 22:37). This means that the command to be teaching our children all the time must not to be interpreted as simply applying to *religious* instruction, set off by itself in an airtight compartment. If our children are not taught to think like Christians when they study math, history, or science, then they are not obeying the command to love God with *all* their minds. And if they are not obeying the command, the parents are held responsible. This is because parents are responsible to instruct their children in what God requires of them. And it must be remembered that Jesus taught us that this is the greatest command—it is the most important one of all. It is clear that God's people, and their children, are required to love the Lord their God with all their *brains*. This involves more than a general acquaintance with David, Goliath, Samson, Noah, *et al.* Sunday School once a week will not get this job done. Nor will family devotions suffice for a few minutes each night.

This second consideration is obviously related to our first, although there is a difference of emphasis. Deuteronomy 6 requires instruction in all of the law, all of the time. The greatest commandment requires the child to receive and love this instruction with all his mind. Because parents are responsible for bringing up children in such a way that they will obey the requirements placed on them by God, it is obvious that the education they provide for their children must teach them to love God in all subject areas. This is not possible when the instructor, school, textbook, and classmates are all in rebellion against God.

A third reason Christian parents are morally obligated to keep their children out of the public schools is because God expects parents to provide for and protect their children. It is truly odd that one of the most common charges made against parents who provide a Christian education for their children is that they are "sheltering" them. What is our nation coming to? Parents sheltering children!

Because pluralism (with regard to worldviews) is a false theology (it is institutional agnosticism), Christian parents are required to protect their children from this lie. Because the public schools are an established institution, required by law to teach and practice agnosticism, Christian parents are obligated to protect children from exposure to this false teaching. The principle is acknowledged by all Christians; it is simply not applied to the

issue of public education by some. It is hard to imagine us
having this debate about Christian kids in Vacation Bible
Schools run by the Jehovah's Witnesses. So why do we
treat agnosticism as a preferable heresy?

Christianity is not the only worldview that pervades
all subjects; false teaching is also equally pervasive. If a
Christian parent attempts to neutralize the false teaching,
it means he has to spend many hours every night counter-
ing what the children learned that day in school. This is
impossible because the parent doesn't know exactly *what*
the children learned that day. And the children themselves
have not been equipped to come back and report on what
was unbiblical in what they heard. They cannot do this
because they have not yet been educated to think like Christians; they cannot do this because they have not been biblically educated. This makes responsible oversight extremely
difficult, and I would argue, impossible. The only alternative is a private Christian education, which a Christian
parent can provide at home or in a Christian school.

Christian parents are morally obligated to keep their
children out of the public schools because sending children into a intellectual, ethical, and religious war zone without adequate training and preparation is a violation of charity.
In a physical war, we know that a country is in desperate
straits when it sends its children to fight. In the same way,
Christianity in this country is in pretty sad shape. We send
our kids off to be warriors, instead of training them to be
warriors. The point is not to keep children from encoun-
ters with those who hate God; rather it is to train and
prepare them for it. We don't send *adults* to the mission
field without training and preparation. But during the time
of training, our children must be protected. What makes
us think that sending unequipped seven-year-olds off to
be "salt and light" in an officially agnostic institution, without
training and preparation, is consistent with charity?

Means for such preparation exist; such preparation is
called *a Christian education*. Once such an education has

been provided by the parents, and the child is truly equipped, he may then be sent into the world. If the parents have done their job, the young adult will be more than a match for anyone he meets.

A fourth consideration is this: Christian parents are morally obligated to keep their children out of the public schools because of the declared intellectual goal assigned to the Church in Scripture. Paul says, "For the weapons of our warfare are not carnal but mighty in God for pulling down strongholds, casting down arguments and every high thing that exalts itself against the knowledge of God, bringing every thought into captivity to the obedience of Christ . . ." (2 Cor. 10:4-5). It is clear to all thinking Christians that the government school system contains many strongholds against the knowledge of God, and many rebellious arguments. Many high things exalt themselves in defiance of God. Our goal as Christians must therefore be to *pull them all down*. Christians who content themselves, in the educational sphere, with anything less than absolute obedience to the Lord Jesus Christ in all areas are consequently compromising this goal given to us in Scripture.

Christian advocates of reform in government education have not vowed that they will settle for nothing less than explicitly *Christian* public schools. Christian reformers generally would settle for "a piece of the action," or a "say" in the great pluralistic discussion. Thus, they do not have conquest, which is the goal of 2 Cor. 10:4-5, in mind. Pluralism (in the realm of world views) is an attempt to make everyone leave everyone else alone; it seeks to make evangelism an offense. But if Christianity is an evangelistic religion (and it is), then such pluralism is an attempt to make Christianity an offense. Christians who agree to the truce which pluralism attempts to impose are being unfaithful to the mission of the Church.

But what if some Christians *do* adopt such a goal of "conquest," *i.e.* they want the public schools to become tax-supported Christian schools? Then such attempts should be resisted for a different reason; God does not assign educational responsibilities to the civil magistrates, even if the magistrates are godly. It is not their area of divinely assigned responsibility.

Fifth, Christian parents are morally obligated to keep their children out of the government schools because the continued presence of Christians subsidizes a lie. Every time the government school doors open, they clearly declare their independence from God in all things. They, officially and on the record, claim the right to teach all their subjects without any submission to God and His Word. Christians who send their children to such schools are subsidizing, with their children as the payment, this particular lie, which we have already discussed. If every Christian parent pulled their children out of the government school system, that school system, along with the lie, would collapse. This means that *Christians* are keeping an institution dedicated to false teaching in existence.

Objections

An initial response to these claims might be that the arguments above are simply arguments for home-schooling, as opposed to private Christian schools. It is true that the arguments above say nothing about home-schools vs. private Christian institutions. While the debate between these two approaches is not incidental, it is primarily a pedagogical discussion, not ethical. The arguments above were geared to whether Christian children should be in *government* schools, and they are arguments with which both home schoolers and Christian school advocates can readily agree.

Another response might be that some Christian schools are poor schools—on both academic and spiritual levels. This is quite true, but it is also beside the point. The question is *not* whether it is morally required to send your child to any and every institution bearing the name "Christian school." Christian parents are not required to say that the corruption of their children is permissible, provided it is done by professing Christians.

There is another possible response, closer to the heart of the matter. This would be to question the claim that government schools are "officially agnostic." Some might want to say that the schools are not agnostic because they are allowed to teach *about* religion, although staying neutral in the teaching *of* religion. Coupled with this, many parents might argue that a "non-agnostic" form of education can be provided by godly parents through a combination of the base education provided at school, mixed with the particular doctrines and beliefs of the parents at home. The picture that comes to mind is the one of how paints are mixed at a paint store. The base paint is neutral, and various colors are added to suit the customer—only in this case the customers mix in their own colors at home.

But if the schools must remain neutral on the teaching *of* religion, how is this not official agnosticism? The schools are allowed to teach *about* religion, true, but does this include the permission to say which one is right? Or is that a detail? And where does Scripture allow us to believe that truth can be learned this way, with a certain percentage of basic, neutral *facts*, which are then mixed with the *truths* of Christianity? The Bible teaches that all truth is God's truth, and none of it is neutral. *There is no such thing as neutrality*. We are therefore kidding ourselves if we think it is possible to provide a godly education for our children by combining Christian ed at home with neutral ed received during the day.

And if Christian parents in the government school system get sufficiently worked up to "take back our schools," this creates questions as well. Do we take the schools back in order to make them *explicitly* Christian, or do we take them back because the secularists cannot be trusted to keep them neutral, while we Christians can keep them neutral? If the former, then are we not formally establishing the Christian religion in a tax-funded institution? Are we not requiring the non-Christians to pay for the propagation of a faith they do not believe? And is this not doing unto them what we do not like done unto us? Moreover this reduces the debate to a question of different *kinds* of Christian education, *i.e.* tax-supported vs. privately-financed. And if it is the latter option, we should ask for the scriptural imperative which requires us to fight to maintain a neutral institution, with a stated mission to propagate neutral facts.

Another objection wonders if it is immoral for Christian parents to send their children to government schools, then is it not equally immoral for them to go out into in the world, rubbing shoulders with all the pagans out there? The biblical answer to this is that we are supposed to be in the world (see, for example, 1 Cor. 5:9-10). But we must be constantly vigilant to see that the world stays out of us, and we must take particular care to keep the world *out of our children*. We must train our children to go into the world; we must not help the world go into our children.

Another question concerns taxes. Whether or not the children of Christians go to government schools, their money most certainly does. Christians should submissively pay their taxes; the taxes are God's chastisement. We are biblically allowed to pay such taxes, because Caesar's image is on what we send them. But *God's* image is on our children, and we are forbidden to render them to Caesar (Mt. 22:21).

Someone else might repudiate the idea of making the government schools explicitly Christian, and maintain that we ought to return to the traditional values of our Western culture, along with a return to academic excellence. To this response, a series of questions and responses comes to mind. First, where does the Bible tell to fight to re-establish Western culture, or traditional values?

Obviously, the Bible is silent when it comes to any such mission. If 2 Cor. 10:4-5 contains a portion of our marching orders, and we should agree it does, then we must note that every thought is to be brought into submission to *Christ*. We are commanded to bring nothing into submission to Wes-tern culture. In the Great Commission, we were not commanded to go into all the earth and make Judeo/Christians, baptizing them in the name of art, music and literature. Western culture at its best is part of the fruit of biblical Christianity, but it must not be confused with it. So if we go into the government schools, and fight for certain "core values," do we do so as Christians, or as plain and ordinary Decent Folks? And what are these core values? Do they include the greatest commandment, *i.e.* that we love the God of Abraham, Isaac and Jacob with everything we have and are? If so, then we are fighting for tax-subsidized Christian schools. If not, then we have abandoned the core of our core values. This dilemma illustrates a central problem in the debate over education—some of our definitions are not the same. Christians should argue that "core values" are those which are at the core of biblical revelation. But many Christians want to argue that "core values" are those which Christians share with decent non-Christians.

But even if the reintroduction of traditional values were our mission, how is it possible to fight for the fruit without fighting for the tree? Our western culture, which many Christians rightly want to protect, did not arrive in our midst *ex nihilo*. It was the result of an explicit affirmation of Christianity proper. There is no problem with the legitimate desire to protect our great heritage, but what is the appropriate means to that end? The tree is the Lord Jesus Christ, and not a traditional morality which is consistent in some general way with Christian morality.

Another possibility is that the general civilizing influence of the government schools could be a precursor to evangelism. Unfortunately, this is backwards. Evangelism results in civilization, and not the other way around. Civilizing moral instruction of this kind does not prepare the ground for saving faith. And even if successful, it is more likely to produce self-righteous moralism than a realization of sinfulness, and need for a Savior. The Bible teaches that sinners are dead in their trespasses and sins. Civilizing "improvements" do not prepare a corpse for life any more than make-up applied by an undertaker prepares a man for the resurrection.

Many agree that the current moral tone in the government schools is horrendous. But this is not what makes them dangerous. We should object, and just as strongly, to officially agnostic government schools which maintain *high* standards of discipline. We must never forget that prostitutes are closer to the kingdom of God than theologians; this is because prostitutes know they have a problem. It is easier to be misled by a false savior before he has fallen on his face. In the same way, it was easier to be mislead by government education before the fruit of that lie became as evident as it has in the last few years. Government education in America in the past had high standards of discipline, *etc.* Consequently, more Christians were deceived at that time than are deceived now. The government schools *then* were more of a threat to the Christian faith.

Conclusion

In closing, it must be said that Christian education is not a luxury, or an option. It is part of Christian discipleship for those who have been blessed with children. Christian education is a necessity because the Bible requires non-agnostic education, because the greatest command includes loving God with all our intellectual capacity, because Christian parents should protect their children from lies, because the goal of the Christian church must be nothing less than intellectual conquest, and because this officially agnostic institution depends for its continued existence on the involvement of professing Christians.

To say Christian parents are morally obligated to provide a Christian education for their children is not necessarily to perpetuate a "spirit of condemnation." It is possible to argue such a position without a legalistic spirit; our desire should be to help parents with their awesome responsibilities, not to weigh them down with extraneous guilt. But to those parents who are working through this crucial issue, this must be said: If these arguments are biblical, then it is necessary to obey them. If not, then it is necessary to answer them.

CHAPTER EIGHT

Love and Security Through Godly Discipline

Discipline and Punishment

We like to paint with a broad brush. In the modern world *discriminating* is a bad word, and so we very rarely are. This is especially true of those areas which bear a superficial resemblance to anything else—whether or not there are profound differences on a more basic level. The difference between discipline and punishment is one such distinction, and one which all diligent parents must master regardless. And so what is the distinction? Discipline is *corrective*; it seeks to accomplish a change in the one being disciplined. Punishment is meted out in the simple interests of justice.

In bringing up children, parents should be disciplining them. In hanging a murderer, the civil magistrate is *not* disciplining—he is punishing. One of the reasons our society is so unsafe is that the magistrate should be punishing, and he isn't; he should not be disciplining, and he is trying to. God disciplines His people as He takes them through the daily process of their sanctification. He has their final glorification in view, and all His discipline works toward that end. But on the last day, He shall punish the wicked. When God finally pitches the ungodly away from Himself, He will have no intention of their subsequent improvement.

Because discipline seeks to correct, *it has accomplished its purpose when the correction has been made*. And because

children are very different, this means that there will be
godly distinctions in the discipline received by various
children. To say it again, kids are different—their person-
alities differ, their attitudes toward pain differ, and of course,
they differ in sex. Consequently, if parents are seeking to
accomplish a particular end through discipline, the amount
of discipline required will vary as the nature of the child
varies. Many parents know what it is like to spank a tough
little tank of a boy, who always tries to make it as far through
a spanking as he can without crying. They also know what
it is like to see their other child dissolve into tears if the
displeased parent looks at her sideways. Parents many times
feel guilty because there is such a disparity in the amount
and intensity of discipline each child receives.

But there is no sound reason for such guilt; it is false
guilt. Compare the problem to one of physical dirt. Suppose some parents have two children, one a dainty girl
who despises getting dirty, and the other a real child of
the soil. Should the parents feel guilty if the second one
gets more baths? Not at all—baths are given according to
need, and so are spankings. Scrubbings are given according to the resistance and tenacity of the grime, and drubbings
are given *on the same principle.* As a result, when a child is
disciplined, it is crucial that the parents avoid the pattern
of "going through the motions." Many Christian parents
have read enough on discipline to know that they are supposed to spank their children, and so they do. But such
spankings can often be seen as nothing more than a mind-
less routine. And why? *The spankings do not achieve the
intended effect.* To return to the analogy of the bath, it is
as though parents knew that well-cared for children take
baths, and so every night they pop the kids into the tub.
They never run the water, and never use soap, but they *do*
get in the tub!

The purpose of *disciplinary* spanking is to alter behavior. If it does not alter the behavior, then the parents
are not applying disciplinary spanking. I have seen

parents spank in astonishing ways. A muffled *wumph* on the diapers, far from eliminating a child's whining, will only increase it. Because the point of discipline is to alter behavior, then ineffective discipline is not really discipline at all. It becomes punishment, and of a bizarre, trifling variety.

The standard for a godly home is simply this—*prompt and cheerful obedience*. This standard, if it is to have any meaning at all, must be enforced whenever there is a violation of the standard. Now the thing that keeps many parents from enforcing such a standard is really their unbelief. They do not believe that discipline will really alter how the kids act around the house. But it does. I have seen parents who were constantly frazzled by their children fighting, squabbling, quarreling, hitting, moaning, and carrying-on, and who put up with it for years on end, when they could put a complete stop to it in three days. All that is needed, to use a phrase my wife and I had, is a short little "reign of terror." This would occur when every infraction was dealt with painfully, every time. The kids catch on.

The objection is that busy parents do not have time to discipline every ten minutes for their rest of their lives. This is where our unbelief is seen. The rest of our lives? Such discipline would be applied for just a few days, and then the home would be transformed. Discipline works. It is used by God to remove folly from the heart of the child. For those parents who seek to be wiser than God, rejecting discipline, nothing awaits their children but a wrenching series of sharp punishments, culminating in the final punishment from the hand of the Lord. Those who refuse to understand discipline *hate their children*. The choice is clear—discipline now or punishment then.

The Manner of Discipline

Because the Bible defines discipline as an act of love, it will only function properly in a broad context of love. It must never be motivated by ungodly anger. In Galatians 6:1, Paul teaches us: "Brethren, if a man is overtaken in any trespass, you who are spiritual restore such a one in a spirit of gentleness, considering yourself lest you also be tempted." This principle is not set aside simply because we are dealing with our children.

We are required by Scripture to correct one another, and this is particularly true in the home. But if we correct someone else, we must be spiritually qualified ourselves. If a parent is angry with his child, he is not spiritual and is therefore disqualified from administering the discipline. If the discipline is administered with a bad attitude, it is not going to be as effective as it would have if it had been calm and judicial—"for the wrath of man does not produce the righteousness of God" (Jas. 1:20). Consequently, a parent cannot bring man's anger toward his children in the act of discipline, and then expect to appropriate the blessings God promised for godly discipline. If he is doing the right thing externally—spanking his children for example—but the manner and disposition of love is missing, it will not have the blessing of God. God does not bless the unrighteous anger of parents.

Equally important is the fact that discipline must not be motivated by embarrassment. There is no question that misbehavior or disobedience by children results in embarrassment at times for parents—"a child left to himself brings shame to his mother" (Prov. 29:15). Lack of discipline *does* result in shame for the parents. But it is crucial that the parents not be motivated to their discipline because of personal embarrassment. One benefit of this is that it keeps children from learning how to manipulate a situation. Children have a real ability for doing the wrong thing at the wrong time. Why do some children throw fits in the supermarket instead of in the kitchen at home? They know that discipline is inconvenient in the supermarket, and that it creates an awkward situation for the parents. But in such situations, children are *not* to be disciplined because they have succeeded in embarrassing their parents. The discipline of the children should not come from the damaged ego of the parents. If a parent is immediately embarrassed, and disciplines because of it, the discipline will not be for the benefit of the child, and, because embarrassment is not constant, the discipline will not be constant either.

The manner of the parent in discipline should be to show that the intention is to restore fellowship between parent and child. But if there is no context of love, then there is no real fellowship to restore. If, after a spanking, the child consistently turns *away* from his parent or runs away, this is an indication that there may be no standing fellowship to restore. If the child turns *back* to his mother or father for comfort after a spanking, that is an indication that there is such standing fellowship. Of course, even well-loved children are sinners, and will be tempted to exhibit this sin through sulking. So if a child ever turns away from his parent, the parent must not immediately assume he is a horrible parent. The child might just want to sulk—and should be disciplined for it. But if that "turning away" is a regular pattern, and the child never turns back to his parents, that should be a danger sign. A home must be a context of love, and discipline is designed to restore the fellowship of that relationship.

Parents should recognize that discipline prevents misbehavior on the part of the child. If a child is not receiving enough attention from his father or mother, and there is no standing context of love, he will often begin to misbehave in order to get attention. Many children operate on the theory "any attention is better than no attention." At school, the children who are running on fumes at home will try to get attention by being popular. If they do not have the capacity to be popular, they undertake a campaign to become unpopular. It is better, they think, to be center-stage and a dork, than to be off-stage,well-behaved, and ignored. *They are unlovely, but at least they are being noticed.*

The natural tendency, even for parents, is to turn away from such an unlovely child, which sends the child further down that road. They get less and less attention, and so they act up more to get more attention. The only real solution to this is for the parents to love *and discipline*. If a father notices his child starting to act up for no apparent reason, he should treat that as a blinking red light which says "My child needs my love and discipline." Parents need to discipline specific misbehavior. But they must also realize if they are getting *more* disobedience and back-chat in return, they need to check whether there is an established and standing context of love. If a child is being neglected and then is disciplined for misbehavior, it is like knocking off bad fruit from a tree, while neglect waters and fertilizes that same tree. Parents must guard against creating what they oppose.

It is not enough to have a context of love surrounding all acts of discipline. The discipline itself is to be done in a loving way. If a parent has the attitude of "Let me at that kid!" and is angry or embarrassed, he is spiritually disqualified to administer the discipline. When the parent is *qualified* to discipline, he probably does not feel like it, and when he feels like it, he is probably not qualified. This is why discipline must be applied in obedience to God's Word, and not in an emotional reaction to a particular situation. The Christian parent must be a biblical parent, not a reacting parent. The rod is to be applied *because God requires it.*

Parents must therefore surround their children with a biblical love. In that environment, sin will still manifest itself, because the child remains a descendant of Adam. But when it does, the parents will deal with it in a context of love—this kind of discipline works. But in a home without love and security, when sin manifests itself, and *then* the parents start whacking away at it, they will simply produce more sin.

The Right Thing at the Right Time

Doing something wrong, or backwards, does not take much preparation or thought. A very common example of this is seen in how many parents think about the transition of their children from infancy to the teenage years. In Proverbs 19:18, it says: "Chasten your son while there is hope, and do not set your heart on his destruction." People fall prey to the illusion created by small cute children. When a child sins, he oftentimes sins in a cute way, and the parents indulge it. When a child first comes into the home, he is small and cute. Although the Bible tells us that we are all sinners by nature, it most certainly does not look this way to us as we are joyfully bending over the crib. Because the child is cute, it is often the case that his sin is "cute" to us as well. Because of this, and because his sin doesn't damage anything much, parents do not discipline effectively for multitudes of "little sins." But the years go by, very quickly, and the parents are soon confronted with a child who is capable of getting pregnant, or getting someone pregnant, getting arrested, buying drugs, and so on. In short, the child is now of sufficient size to wreck his life. In a panic, his parents attempt to institute a regime of strict discipline. Not surprisingly, this provokes even more rebellion. What has gone wrong?

Parents often think the teen years are a time to *start* imposing standards. But when a child is older, that should be the time when the standards are *lifted*, and not imposed. If the child has been properly disciplined when he is young, he will be self-controlled and responsible. He should not have any rules remaining by the time he is sixteen or seventeen. If the parent feels that there must be rules at this time, that simply means that not enough standards were imposed when he was younger.

If a home is governed by *rules, rules, rules* when the young man is seventeen years old, how will he maintain a standard of godliness when he leaves home at eighteen? The parents will not be able to restrain him when he joins the U.S. Navy, and has a home-port somewhere in Japan. But if he has been formed and taught properly when he was young, when he is old, he will not depart from the way his parents taught him (Prov. 22:6).

"And you, fathers . . . bring them up in the training and admonition of the Lord" (Eph. 6:4). Paul says that fathers are to bring their children up in the training and admonition of the Lord. The verb translated here as *bring up* also means to *nourish up to maturity*, or *nurture*. This requires intelligent oversight of the entire growing process. The goal of child-rearing must be Christian maturity displayed in our children. This goal must be in the minds of the parents long before it is reached. It must be in mind from the beginning.

The Bible requires fathers to exercise this kind of intelligent oversight of their children *as they grow*. The critical years in this process are the early ones. An oak sapling can be bent with very little effort; if fifty years are added, it will be an entirely different story. So why do so many Christian parents let the saplings in their homes grow without strict pruning, and then try to shape the tree only after all the problems with their folly are manifest in the form of a huge twisted oak? The answer is that many Christian fathers are foolishly disobeying Ephesians 6:4. Instead of loose tolerance when the kids are little, and clamping down as they grow older, a biblical approach is just the reverse. As stated earlier, small children should live in a "totalitarian police state" at home. "Foolishness is bound up in the heart of a child, but the rod of correction will drive it far from him" (Prov. 22:15). The smaller a child is, the more decisions should be made for him.

Conversely, the older the children are, the *fewer* the

external restrictions there should be. As a child is being reared properly, he should experience greater and greater freedom. This is possible because early strict discipline works and has by now been internalized. The easy mistake to make is that of indulging children when they are small and cracking down on them as they grow. Instead of this, parents should be super-strict with little ones and gradually remove restrictions as the children mature. The teenage years are no time to institute strict discipline. In other words, when a child is small, he should not be burdened with responsibilities. When a child is older, he should not be burdened with restrictions.

When our children were young, we would discipline for things that many would consider "little." For example, one infraction that could bring about a spanking would be whining. This might cause some readers to roll their eyes heavenward—"If we disciplined for whining, we would have to discipline every ten minutes for the next twenty years!" The first part is quite true—one might have to do this every ten minutes, especially if there has been parental indulgence of the sin of whining. But it does not have to be done for twenty years. It only has to be done consistently for two or three days, at which time the whining will stop.

Many parents might wonder, however, whether their two-year-old can understand the connection between the discipline and the whining. This concern can be addressed with a simple question—does this two-year-old understand the connection between his whining and whatever it is he wants? The answer of course is *yes*. Such an understanding is why he whines. This means that the child is fully capable of understanding the nature of cause and effect, and is therefore capable of understanding the discipline. The reason he still whines is because he has not been disciplined for it.

Obviously, this should not be done from some dictatorial need to boss kids around. This kind of strict discipline when children are little is self-sacrificial. It is much easier on "self" to let things go. The purpose of such discipline is so that it will not be necessary to exercise strict discipline later, after it has become extremely difficult—or impossible.

Although we disciplined for many "small" things, as our children have grown, we have given them greater and greater freedom as we have seen them mature. For example, when the children were younger, we had strict standards concerning entertainment. There have been many times when our younger children were not permitted to watch a movie that other Christian kids were watching—on video at a birthday party, for example. But when our oldest daughter was sixteen, we told our her that she was now free to make her own decisions on whether to watch a film with her friends or not. There was no longer any need to "phone home." We did not do this because objectionable movies were now all right to watch (they are not), but because we can now trust her to make good choices. The irony is that she now has been given a much greater freedom in this than many of her friends from less strict homes.

The sum of the matter is this. When other young children are cruising the neighborhood without restraint, your children should be at their home—Camp Pendleton. And ten years later, when the kids in the neighborhood are all getting grounded, yours should finally be getting airborne.

The Husband & Wife Team

An important part of a child's security comes from Christian parents learning to discipline *together* on the basis of the authority that God has given to them. They are invested with *authority*. Paul tells us in Ephesians 6:1-4 that the central authority is given to fathers. At the same time, mothers are usually very interested in the implementation of godly discipline. It is therefore important for him to invest authority in her. When dad comes home in the evening after being away at work, the children will usually mind him after having given their mother trouble all day. He should not say to his frazzled wife, "What is *your* problem?"

Once I was talking to a man who pointed this out while boasting over his wife. He said something like, "I really discipline the kids well, but my wife can't control them." He was talking as though he were winning a competition with her. But if he is disciplining them and she is not, the end result will be undisciplined children, and it is *his* problem. Consequently, whenever children are dealing with their mother, they should see behind their mother the looming shadow of their father. It does not matter if he is on the other side of the country. Dad should invest his full authority in her and back her up completely. Whether the father is physically in the home or not, he is still responsible for the discipline. He is to come to his wife and solicit information from her on how the day went. He should not have to wait for her to get to such a high level of frustration that she dumps it on him.

So the husband's perception of home life is not to be limited to what he sees; he must communicate with his wife. He needs to be in communication with the teachers of his children. Fathers are responsible to see to it that their children are well disciplined *all the time.* This is a command from God. If they are brought up in the training and admonition of the Lord, then the fathers will have done their job. A father cannot come up before God when He calls him to account for how his children ended their lives and excuse himself by saying, "If my wife had only been a stricter disciplinarian . . ." *If she needs to be stricter, he must see to it.* He must give her more authority, strength, and support.

Many times the wife is doing everything God expects of her. When she spanks, the spanking is painful, and when she corrects, the correction is prompt and strict. But, if her husband is not backing her up, the impact she is going to have on her children is going to be far less than if he were supporting her. When our children were little, my wife disciplined them more frequently than I because she was around them more during the day. She knows how to spank, and she did it right. At the same time, the children tended to pay more attention to me. Some would say that this does not make any sense—the person that should be feared is the one who exercises the most discipline. But God has vested the foundational authority in the home with the father. Consequently, the father should self-consciously assume that role and should support his wife fully. I can still remember very clearly the three big "No's" when I was growing up: lying, disobedience, *and disrespect of our mother*. My father backed my mother up completely.

Discipline in the Christian home should be conducted over time with an appropriate sense of urgency. Eternal things depend upon what we do, as well as whether our children end their lives in temporal ruin. By urgency, I do not mean panic, stress, or anxiety; it must be intelligent, focused, biblical urgency. Mothers are commonly tempted to an inappropriate anxiety. They tend to take the rearing of their children more "seriously" than husbands do, and this brings a separate set of temptations with it. Oftentimes, if it is late and the wife is tired and finally has a moment to herself, she is tempted to think, *Oh, I am a rotten mother; my kids are not obeying me properly . . . .* If she then starts trying to discipline her children from a sense of anxiety, she will be doing it incorrectly.

CHAPTER NINE

The Application of Godly Discipline

A Scenario

"I have a problem," Steven said.

"What's that?" Robert looked up from his coffee. The two were co-workers, and had decided to have lunch together.

"It's my kids. I've got two boys, both pre-school age, and they are driving my wife up the wall. And, to be honest, she's driving *me* up the wall."

"How come?"

"Our standards are different. She has higher standards for the kids with regard to how they *behave*, and I have higher standards about what constitutes actual *discipline*."

"So she is frustrated with how infrequently you discipline, and concerned about how strict you are when you do?"

"Right . . . Listen, the reason I wanted to talk with you is because of *your* kids. They are older than mine, but whenever I am around them, I'm impressed with how well-behaved they are. Did your kids go through this stage? Will they grow out of it?"

Robert laughed. "Yes, my kids went through this stage. But the stage is not called the *terrible two's*. The stage is called *sin*. And kids won't grow out of it—they grow more and more *into* it—unless they are disciplined in a biblical way."

"Okay. I'm listening."

"The biggest problem with parents of kids your age is that the parents expect *far too little from them*."

"What do you mean?"

"They think that a two-year-old, for example, can't understand that whining is wrong."

Steven's eyes got wide. "You disciplined for *whining*?"

Robert laughed. "Certainly."

"But if *we* disciplined for whining, we would be discipling them all day long, every day . . ."

". . . for a couple of days. Then the whining would stop."

Steven sat back in the booth. "Go on."

"This is what I mean by low expectations. You said that your wife had higher standards than you did, but   neither of you have standards which are high enough. Because of that you both put up with behavior which   neither of you like. After a while, you get to your boiling point, and wham! discipline occurs. But it is not effective discipline, because it is occuring far too late in the game. It is the disciplinary equivalent of a Hail Mary pass."

"So you are saying that kids that age can understand the connection between the whining and the discipline?"

"Of course they can. Can they understand the connection between the whining and whatever it is they want?"

"Yes, they sure do that."

"So what makes you think that when it comes to what *you* require of them, they immediately become stupid?"

Steven thought for a moment. "You know, I really don't know. What you are saying is obvious. Why haven't we seen it?"

"I can't say for sure, but there is one strong possibility."

"What is that?"

"Disciplining your kids according to a high standard is hard work. Not doing it is easier. Postponing discipline until some crisis comes along is easy on the flesh."

"Okay, I have two questions then. The first is, how do we set this high standard?"

"When it comes to attitudes and external behavior based on those attitudes, your standards for your kids should be the same as the biblical standards for mature Christians."

"You can't be serious."

"I'm dead serious. You don't discipline for *physical* immaturity—clumsy motor skills which result in a spilled glass of milk, for example. But everything which is morally objectionable in adults should be disciplined for in children."

"Like . . .?"

"Like rudeness, tale-bearing, whining, complaining, ingratitude, envy, temper, cheating, laziness, lying, name-calling, pride, resentment, stealing, and back-chat. For starters."

Steven was shaking his head. "My wife is not going to believe this."

"What was your second question?"

"How can you be sure this will work?"

"There are three reasons I am sure."

"They are . . .?"

"God, in His Word, tells parents to do it this way. According to the Bible, disciplining children *works*. The second reason is just common sense."

"What do you mean by that?"

Robert leaned over and tapped the table in front of Steven. "My philosophy of child-rearing is very simple. You are *bigger* than they are. If what they are doing is wrong, *make them stop*."

Steven laughed. "And what is your third reason?"

"I have seen it work. My children are all descendants of Adam, just like yours. They were no less prone to sin than yours. But we sought to obey God in how we brought up our children, and He has blessed it. We are very grateful."

"Yes, but . . ." Steven stopped.

Robert smiled. "I know what you were going to say."

Steven looked up with a half-smile. "What was I going to say?"

"You were going to say that it is all very well for us, because we were fortunate enough to get good kids."

"Okay. But you *do* have good kids."

"But not by accident. Suppose a man has a garden, but he is knee-deep in weeds. He looks across the fence and sees his neighbor with nothing but vegetables. Can he say that it is all very well, but that his neighbor's garden doesn't have weeds in it? It doesn't have weeds for a *reason*."

Steven nodded his head. "Makes sense."

Robert leaned back and laughed. "Do you want to hear a story I heard once? It's a true story . . . a friend of mine and his wife were visiting his folks, who objected very strongly to the spanking of their precious grandson. Well, their little grandson got into trouble somehow, and was taken off to the bedroom for his spanking. When Dad came back, his folks just let him have it—'What do you mean, spanking our grandson?' But one of the reasons they offered for not spanking him was really revealing. They said he should not be spanked *because he was the most well-behaved grandchild they had*. That was quite true, but it was true for a reason."

Steven thought for a moment. "My kids aren't going to know what is happening to them."

"They'll catch on soon enough."

"This will involve lots of spanking."

Robert smiled. "Yes, it will. There were times when my wife spent the whole day with a wooden spoon in her hip pocket. But in the long run you wind up disciplining far *less*."

Steven leaned forward. "Okay, that brings up another point. Remember I mentioned that I had a stricter view of what constitutes discipline? Well, my wife has trouble spanking our kids. This sounds funny, but I think she needs spanking lessons."

"That is a common enough problem. But you can teach her. If you are taking responsibility for the whole area of child-discipline, I think she will respect your teaching in this."

"Well, I need help there too. What can you tell me about teaching her to spank? What are some basic rules of spanking?"

"There are four basic rules."

"Okay, what's the first?"

"Never spank in anger. Don't discipline for *your* sake, but rather for the child's. The discipline should be judicial and calm. This is one area where high standards help. High standards mean that you will discipline when you are not emotionally close to the edge. If you only discipline when your kids are guilty of some outrage, it is harder to control your anger."

"The second?"

"Discipline must be painful. It must not inflict damage, so use a *flat* wooden spatula. At the same time it must inflict *pain*—memorable pain. Don't spank over diapers. Don't spank with a little tap, tap, tap. Teach your wife to flick her wrist when she spanks, and teach her to think *sting*. There are many parents who go through the motions of spanking, but they are not really spanking."

"How can you tell?"

"By whether or not the child's behavior changes."

"What is the third thing?"

"Spanking should be a time of instruction. The child should know what the offense was and that the Bible teaches against the offense. He shouldn't think he is being spanked because he got on *your* nerves."

"And the last?"

"When the spanking is over, there must be a full restoration of fellowship. The child should be loved and held until the crying is over. Then you should pray with him; it should be fixed in his mind that God has used the spanking to cleanse him. They are forgiven; the subject is closed."

"Do you really think we can do all this?"

"I certainly know that you *can*. Because there is hard work and self-discipline involved, it is up to you whether or not you *will*."

"Thanks. I am sure we'll have questions. Can I talk to you again sometime?"

"Anytime."

The Mechanics of Discipline

Reference was made above to the ineffectual nature of many spankings. This brings us to the subject of the *mechanics* of child discipline. This is where the rubber meets the road, or, if we abhor cliches, where the wood meets the bottom. Perhaps some people who are sensitive on the subject of child abuse, or who have been abused themselves, cringe when they hear jokes like this about spanking. But one of the ways a person can tell whether there is a context of love in the home is in whether or not the children appreciate such humor. If they have enjoyed a context of love in the home, the rod is not something that is frightening to them at all. If a biblical home is functioning the way it should, and a child has been disciplined effectively, then that child has no problem understanding the need for discipline. They see it as a loving thing to do.

Children must be disciplined because there is an eternal consequence to sin which is far more grievous than the pain of a spanking. When parents spank their child, they are placing obstacles between the child and hell, which is the child's destiny apart from the gracious intervention of God. God uses godly parents as one of His means of intervening. Proverbs 23:13-14 says: "Do not withhold correction from a child, for if you beat him with a rod, he will not die. You shall beat him with a rod, and deliver his soul from hell." Many tender parents are afraid of overdoing the discipline. Many Christian parents are very tender-hearted, gentle, kind, and love their children very much.

But they are afraid that if they spank their children *too much*, they are going to cross the line into child abuse. But the division between godly spanking and child abuse is *not* a nebulous gray area. Christians should have very little patience with the impression of child abuse created by humanistic social workers, which virtually considers abuse as *anything* unpleasant happening to a child. But the two are as different as night and day. There is a stark difference between sharp discipline applied in a context of love, and self-centered child abuse. The world and its propaganda machine warn that we have to be very careful about this and not go "too far." Their message blurs the distinction between abuse and biblically mandated discipline.

Christians need to be reminded that if they apply the rod to their child, it will not kill him, and that they need not be afraid to lay it on. They should not have pity on their child in the short-term, but rather they should pity their child over the course of his life. The child is not capable of comprehending long-term consequences. Chikdren do comprehend, and do not like, sharp, short-term discipline, which is the whole point. The parent should not be afraid of overdoing *biblical* obedience. Christian parents who are in the greatest fear of overdoing it, are, in fact, in grave danger of underdoing it. And this is fatal in an eternal way.

The text in Proverbs says, "Do not withhold correction." This leaves us as parents with an obligation to find out the elements of that correction, and then diligently to apply it. Parents can withhold correction from the children in one of two ways. One is not to do anything, and the other is to go through the biblical motions, but to actually accomplish nothing.

The first thing to note is that effective discipline is painful. Hebrews 12:11 says it this way: "Now no chastening seems to be joyful for the present, but painful; nevertheless, afterward, it yields the peaceful fruit of righteousness to those who have been trained by it."

Short-term discipline is painful. The long-term result of discipline is the peaceful fruit of righteousness. Short-term peace in the home can be purchased by not disciplining. "I just got home from work, I'm tired and I don't want a scene. I don't want to spank my child. I want a half hour of peace, and I am willing to purchase this peace with my child suffering the long-term consequences." If it is effective discipline, it is going to be painful and unpleasant. If it is not painful, it is not discipline. Many Christian parents do not really spank, but simply go through the motions—*tippy, tap, tippy, tap*—on the top of the diapers. It does not take the child very long to figure out this does not hurt. When there is no pain in discipline, there is a chronic unpleasantness in the home rather than acute pain. Discipline must be a memorable event; it is not effective as a low-grade unpleasantness.

Sharp discipline is far more effective when there has been an atmosphere of pleasantness in the home. This atmosphere of pleasantness needs to be punctuated from time to time with pain. For example, even though we might want a pleasant evening with our guests rather than have to discipline our child, we must always contrast the short-term and long-term consequences. If the child is not disciplined immediately, parents will never enjoy any pleasant evenings with any guests.

Mothers are tempted to resort to threats and nagging, "I am warning you, wait until your father gets home . . ." But the father is tempted to neglect discipline as well—he doesn't want to sort through fifteen different offenses over the course of the day, and so he trades in long-term godly consequences for a dearly bought short-term peace in the home.

If pain is being delivered effectively, in most situations, *three to five swats are sufficient*. If it is major confrontation, five to ten swats may be in order. If the parents are spanking more than that on a consistent basis, then they are disciplining *incorrectly*. One time my wife got a phone call from someone who was delivering a great number of swats to a little child, and nothing was happening. There were no results; there was no correction in the child's behavior. The parent's arm was going through the air enough times, but there was no pain being delivered.

When children are grown, they should be able to remember what the pain was like from certain spankings. They may not be able to remember what the spanking was for, because spankings cleanse and forgiveness follows, but the pain should be memorable. There must be pain in a good spanking, but no damage. A child abuser will inflict pain *and* damage, but this is not biblical discipline. But most Christian parents inflict neither pain nor damage. This is not discipline either. A spanking should be the kind of thing that the child is unwilling to receive again. If a parent feels he is pounding his child and not making any difference, then he should seek spanking lessons from parents who are getting results. Parents should think to "sting" their children, as opposed to clobbering them. When the child is stung, there is much pain and no damage.

Another important component in effective discipline is *consistency*. If the standards are only enforced on Tuesdays and every second Wednesday, then the child is only being taught how capricious his parents are. These standards clearly cannot be biblical because they are only enforced sometimes. If they were God's standards they would be enforced all the time. Instead, the children learn to think that discipline proceeds from Dad's quirkiness. "Sometimes this misbehavior is a big deal, and other times it is not a big deal at all." The child is being taught that his parents are arbitrary, and not that there is a standard that is fixed and immovable. Discipline should occur for those things that God requires, and not intermittently, as the parent feels like it.

However, it is not enough that discipline be painful and consistent. Effective discipline must also be proportioned to the offense. If the punishment does not fit the crime, there will be a great likelihood that the child will become discouraged. "Fathers, do not provoke your children, lest they become discouraged" (Col. 3:21). Fathers need to take great care that they do not provoke their children through tyrannical discipline. Parents must also remember that the definition of proportionality should come from the *Scriptures*, and not from their own upbringing. For example, is lying a big deal in Scripture? The answer is *yes*—when a child is speaking to his parent, there is no such thing as a white lie. Is whining a spankable offence? God disciplined the Hebrew children in the wilderness for their *grumbling*. Because of our connection to Adam, children will start grumbling as soon as they figure out how. The parents must respond, "In God's book, complaining and grumbling and whining were not permitted," and then the child must be disciplined for it.

Discipline should be more intense for outright defiance and rebellion than it would be for other offenses. One time when my son was around two he had his "big wheel" across the street. I called over to him and said, "Nathan, I don't want you riding that in the street."

He said, "But I want to."

"I don't want you to." I replied.

He said, "I'm gonna." And he took off.

Now of course I was not out there asking for a showdown, but when there was a direct challenge to my authority, I had to treat it as a major offense. The spanking should be proportional.

If a child's bad attitude is being corrected, Mom should say something like, "No grumbling," using the name the family has for the sin (whining, fussing, etc.), and if the child continues *any longer*, he must be spanked. "You can't do that in this house. You are not allowed to grumble." At the same time, the spanking should be proportioned to the offense.

Related to this is the truth that effective discipline is within reason. In Psalm 103:13-14, the Lord says: "As a father pities his children, so the Lord pities those who fear Him. For He knows our frame, he remembers that we are dust." As our Heavenly Father, the Lord takes our frame into account and remembers that we are dust. Earthly fathers are to make sure they realize what their children's abilities are and what they are not. Many parents believe that their child has far *less* understanding than the child actually has. Sometimes parents go to the other extreme and assume the child has far more ability and understanding. Children are not to be disciplined for childishness or immaturity. But frequently, those are the things for which parents are tempted to discipline—because the physical immaturity irks them or gets under their skin. Spilling the milk, wetting the bed, *etc.*, are things that the child cannot usually help. But if the child is spanked anyway, he may think to himself, "I got spanked for doing this and I cannot help it." His frame is not being considered or thoughtfully remembered.

Suppose a child is walking through the living room, trips, knocks over the lamp and breaks it—pure accident. There should not be any discipline beyond a calm admonition to be more careful in the future. But if he had been told five minutes before to stop throwing the ball in the living room, and he continued to do so, knocked the lamp over and broke it, then he must be spanked clearly and decisively. This is not because of the lamp, but because of the disobedience to his parents.

Suppose a child in a certain circumstance is told to do something, and he says, "Yes, mother," and then he runs off to do it. But then some situation comes up which distracts him from obedience. In a situation like that, the parent should remind him of his responsibility to follow through and perform the required task. An appropriate word quietly spoken may deal with the situation. But over an extended period of time, the child will probably begin saying, "I forgot," as an excuse or defense. At this point he should be spanked for the forgetfulness. Such discipline helps a child with his memory skills. We tend to think that forgetting is a reasonable excuse, whereas in Scripture it is an additional offense. "They forgot God their Savior, Who had done great things in Egypt, wondrous works in the land of Ham, awesome things by the Red Sea" (Ps. 106:21-22).

Another important aspect of discipline is that it must be administered *quickly*. Moreover, the younger the child is the more important it is that the discipline be swift. When he is really young, a long time between the offense and the discipline will make it difficult for him to realize what the spanking was for. If a toddler wants to put electric plugs into his mouth, he cannot be told, "You did that three times today and I am going to have your father spank you when he gets home." Discipline must obviously occur right away. With regard to criminal justice, Ecclesiastes says, "Because the sentence against an evil work is not executed speedily, therefore the heart of the sons of men is fully set in them to do evil" (Eccl. 8:11). In a similar way, the discipline of children must be prompt and immediately associated with the sin. The discipline must be swift and efficient. Many parents undercut this with an early warning system for their children. *I am going to count to ten.* The children are simply being trained to count, and to obey at nine. If the parent gets to eight and the child says to himself, "Okay, I have to obey within two seconds," could not that two seconds have been earlier in the count? When the child hears nothing but *I'm warning you!* he is being trained to disobey, or obey only when the parent gets to a certain decibel level. This is not how it should be.

The Scriptures should be applied to every situation and expounded regularly. Certain phrases should be repeated in the home so often that they stay with the child through life. If the child has been disciplined effectively, he will one day be heard saying the same things to *his* children. For example, one of the things I often heard growing up, and which we have taught our children and hope they will in turn teach their children, is "Delayed obedience is disobedience." It should be repeated and driven home; it should be enforced in a context of love; the children should learn it. Then they will teach their children the same way.

Another aspect of effective discipline is that it cannot be *prolonged*. Pleasantness should reign in the biblical home, and discipline should be a brief event. But in many homes chronic unpleasantness reigns all the time. When discipline occurs, it is simply a matter of going from bad to worse. Godly discipline is not like that; of course there will be acute unpleasantness from time to time during the discipline, but an atmosphere of joy and peace and graciousness reigns *most* of the time. If the parents are turning discipline into a long, drawn-out process, they are not disciplining the way God instructed. This trap frequently catches parents of older children. At a certain age the children get too big to spank without abusing their dignity. But they still need to be disciplined. If they were spanked effectively when they were little, then other forms of discipline will be quite effective.

There is a popular form of discipline for teenagers which appears to meet this need, but which has its problems. It is called *grounding*. When a teenager is grounded, the result is frequently two weeks of unpleasantness in the home. But the purpose of discipline is to *restore* pleasantness to the home. All too often grounding says, "You can't go out and do that; you have to stay here and mope." Suppose they start to mope and are told, "You can't mope." They can think, "Well, what are you going to do if I do anyway—ground me?" If the teenager is grounded and not pleased with the discipline, unhappiness is going to remain in the home.

The heart of the New Covenant is centered around forgiveness of sins. We are all forgiven sinners. If children are reminded of their failing on a daily basis for two

weeks, then they are going to become discouraged because they are being taught a doctrinal falsehood. The parents
are saying that what Isaiah said was false when he wrote,
"Come let us reason together, though your sins be as scarlet,
they shall be as white as snow." The purpose of spanking
is for the children to be cleansed, and when they are clean,
the sin is gone. When the "grounded" teenager has an attitude problem and grounding cannot be put on top of grounding, the relationship has been disrupted. But the whole
purpose of discipline is to *restore* the relationship between
parents and children.

So if the child is too old to spank, but still needs
discipline, the biblical pattern for such discipline is restitution. If the older child has done something that needs
discipline, some kind of restitution should be required.
The restitution should be directed to the person against
whom he has sinned. The restitution may require money
(to pay for a damaged item, for example) or can be as mild
as a required formal apology. A required apology is particularly effective with boys. In this regard, boys can be
very prideful. When a boy has sinned against someone else,
nothing goes right to the heart of the matter quite as effectively as requiring him to humble himself in the sight
of the person he wronged. It is important not to let him
off with a little note that says, "Sorry." Sorry for what?
Sorry for doing it? Sorry it happened? Sorry he got caught?
He should be made to state what the offense was, say he
was wrong for doing it, and ask for forgiveness. He will
be in agony while he is doing it, but when it is done, it is
done.

But it is important to remember that if children are
being spanked effectively when they are *little*, the parents
will not have monumental problems trying to figure out
what to do when they are teenagers. The parental authority must be established and fixed when the children
are young. Discipline should fix the problem. When our
oldest daughter was a toddler, there was one day when

her attitude was just plain bad, and even though she had done nothing *exactly* disobedient, she certainly was walking right down the line. She was pushing it. I remember saying to my wife that we should look for an opportunity to spank her. Of course, it was not long before she was spanked. What followed was a wonderful illustration for me as a young parent of what discipline was supposed to *do*. That night, after she was spanked and restored, I could not believe how happy she was—she was dancing around the house. Her sins were gone, and she was forgiven.

If the child is undisciplined, unconfessed sin is accumulating and weighing him down. "[L]et us lay aside every weight, and the sin which so easily ensnares us, and let us run with endurance the race that is set before us . . ." (Heb. 12:1) If parents do not discipline, they are letting such weight accumulate on their children. If there is a context of love, the bigger the pile gets, the more the child is going to feel out of fellowship with his parents. But when the child is disciplined, the sin is dealt with, and there is *joy*.

Discipline can be understood as either active or passive. The bulk of visible discipline will be active, but there is a place for thoughtful passive discipline, particularly in the case of really young children. Passive discipline occurs when a decision is made by parents *not* to intervene. For example, what should be done when it is time for bed? The baby is fed and changed, and put to bed, but in bed he yells and yells. When the parents tell the child to count it all joy when he meets various trials, and then leave him there in bed, that is passive discipline. Children should be passively disciplined from the time they come home from the hospital. Active discipline occurs when parents intervene to apply *artificial* consequences for the improper behavior. There are many features to active discipline which are important for parents to master. The neglect of any one of these features will hinder the effectiveness of the discipline and water it down.

In summary, the mode should be biblical. "Do not withhold correction from a child, for if you beat him with a rod, he will not die. You shall beat him with a rod, and deliver his soul from hell" (Prov. 23:13-14). The application of discipline should be also painful. There are many Christian parents, particularly mothers, who render the proper mode of discipline useless through half-hearted or timid application. "Now no chastening seems to be joyful for the present, but painful; nevertheless, afterward it yields the peaceable fruit of righteousness to those who have been trained by it" (Heb. 12:11). If discipline is not painful, it is not discipline. At the same time, discipline must be proportionate and within reason. The right attitude is seen in the Psalms. "As a father pities his children, so the Lord pities those who fear Him. For He knows our frame; He remembers that we are dust" (Ps. 103:13-14). The same kind of thing is seen in the warning found in the New Testament: "Fathers, do not provoke your children, lest they become discouraged" (Col. 3:21).

The discipline must be consistent. The Bible teaches that discipline *teaches*. So if discipline is erratic and capricious, it is *teaching lies*. Consistent strict discipline also protects the parent from disciplining in anger—which parents should *never* do—"the wrath of man does not produce the righteousness of God" (Jas. 1:20). Parents who "feel like" disciplining, whose emotions are really into it, are not qualified. "Brethren, if a man is overtaken in any trespass, you who are spiritual should restore such a one in a spirit of gentleness, considering yourself lest you also be tempted" (Gal. 6:1). The pattern set down generally for correction in the church would certainly also apply in the home. Parents who are spiritual are qualified to discipline, but probably don't feel like it. Parents who feel like it are probably not qualified. The solution is for qualified parents to discipline out of obedience to God, and not from an emotional reaction.

The discipline must be swift. The younger the child,

the swifter it must be. At the same time, remember the previous principle that parents should make sure the discipline is applied with the swiftness *of principle*, not the swiftness of temper. Small children do have short memories, and they must know why they are being disciplined.

Fundamentally, parents must act as though they believe discipline *works*. And because the point of discipline is to correct and restore the child, parents must actively restore fellowship after the discipline. The procedure should be something like this: explain the offence, and why Scripture teaches that it is wrong; spank the child; hold and comfort the child until the crying is done; explain to the child that all is forgiven; and then pray with the child.

The Bible promises nothing for nominal disciplinarians. If a parent withholds correction, or disciplines ineffectively, there is no promise concerning the children. There is no promise unless they discipline lovingly, consistently and biblically. If parents just go through the motions and then look for godly offspring, they will be disappointed. Biblical discipline is painful, consistent, proportionate, considerate, swift, and not prolonged. If discipline is administered in this way, keeping in mind the promises discussed in earlier chapters, there can be an assurance from God. He will fulfill His promise to these parents, as they love the Lord their God with all their hearts, and as they do so in their family.

The Occasions of Discipline

When discipline is exercised, the parent should bring the authority of *God* to bear on the child's disobedience. In *Withhold Not Correction*, Bruce Ray has pointed out how Paul teaches children their biblical obligations in Ephesians 6:

> • He first *addresses* the children directly.
> • He then *states* the principle: "Obey your parents in the Lord. . . ."

• He *applies* the Word, "Honor your father and mother. . . ."
• He *explains* the Word, "which is the first commandment with a promise. . . ."

This approach should be equally clear to our children. We are tempted to govern by threatening: *Stop that. If you do that one more time, I am going to . . .!* But it is wrong to be nebulous with threats because it leaves the sorting out of *why* and *why not* to the child. If the parent can't come up with a relevant biblical passage for having Johnny stop whatever it is, then there should be a very real question about why it is such a big deal. At the same time, if sin is addressed biblically in the household, then obedience, disobedience, anger, confession, envy, laziness, lying, name-calling, stealing, tattling will all be addressed.

Suppose a child is tattling, taking great glee and no small pride in being on the right side of an issue. The parent should address the child like this:

> Billy, I want you to stop tattling on your sister. God says, "Where there is no wood, the fire goes out; and where there is no talebearer, strife ceases" (Prov. 26:20). Do you want to know why you are in fights with your sister all the time? We have a wood stove. What would happen in the winter if we never put wood on the stove? The fire would die out, wouldn't it? What would happen if you would quit tattling on your sister? The arguments would die out. That is what the Word of God says.

The child has been addressed and told what is expected for him to do, where the Bible says to do it, and then the teaching of Scripture has been explained to him. This enables the child to see that these requirements are not arbitrary rules that his parents have made up out of blue sky. A parent can be a strict disciplinarian without being a biblical disciplinarian. But usually such strictness results in a confusion between house rules and God's rules.

By What Standard?

When we think about how we live our lives, and we seek to make decisions, we are constantly confronted with the question—"By what standard?" The question confronts us in the area of discipline as well. Christian parents must diligently seek to see that the heart of their standards are grounded in the Word of God. The Bible does not leave parents stranded on this crucial issue. Parents must obey and apply the Word. It is important to remember that this is *not* the same thing as setting standards according to denominational traditions, or popular evangelical taboos.

It is also important to keep in mind the fact that the Bible does *not* set different ethical standards based on age. When the law was given on Mt. Sinai, it was not given for adults only. On the contrary, we should consider the breadth of the law given in Deuteronomy 5:1-21. If we turn to the next chapter, we see the instruction given to *parents* there. All the words spoken by God were to be taught to the children (Deut. 6:4-9). If we turn to the next chapter we can see the result of faithful parental instruction. "Therefore know that the LORD your God, He is God, the faithful God who keeps covenant and mercy for a thousand generations with those who love Him and keep His commandments . . ." (Deut. 7:9). So in the area of moral behavior, moral attitudes, *etc.*, parents should make *no* allowances for age. Sin is sin, whether it is mature or immature. The ethical expectations for small children should be identical to those which we have for mature Christian adults. Of course, small children should not be disciplined for physical, mental, or emotional immaturity, but sin is in another category *altogether*.

As parents grow in their understanding of God's requirements, they will be able to sharply distinguish house rules from God's rules. Every household must make decisions on how it will function. As Christians, the moral standards are already set for us; our job is to study the Scriptures to find out what they already are. But there are other issues, on which parents must make a decision, and concerning which the Bible provides no explicit instruction. Consequently, parents should make sure the children are instructed on the difference between rules they have made for the home, and rules God has made for the home.

For example, God's rules forbid lying, and so it must be forbidden in every Christian home. House rules may forbid jumping on the couch. The rules rest upon a different foundation (human wisdom, not divine commandment). If parents are not careful in instructing the children in terms of this distinction, the children could easily wind up legalistic, or rebellious.

. Parents should also understand that if they learn to discipline for "trivial" things, then they will not have to discipline for great transgression. "Who can understand his errors? Cleanse me from secret faults. Keep back Your servant also from presumptuous sins; let them not have dominion over me. Then I shall be blameless, and I shall be innocent of great transgression" (Ps. 19:12-13). In the same way, parents should protect their children from presumptuous sinning (through consistent discipline) as a means of protecting them from a great fall. *Big oaks come from little acorns.* No overwhelming problem in child-rearing *started out* overwhelming. In every case, it was allowed to *grow* to crisis proportions from very small beginnings. Many of the more common "little" sins which are frequently left undisciplined are whining, squabbling, slow obedience, tale-bearing, laziness, disrespect, and, of course, much more.

Parents must not lead their children into temptation. Our heavenly Father minimizes temptation for us; we must do the same for our children (Mt. 6:13; 1 Cor. 10:13). For example, parents should not keep them up to all hours, and then marvel when they are crabby. Parents must not issue commands like a machine gun, and then wonder why all the commands are not obeyed. Parents are to imitate God, not some tyrannical agency of the federal government. Parents must pick their battles carefully, and then win *all* the battles.

It is also a good idea to prepare children for times of temptation. Each family knows when the times of testing are. They may involve a desperate hunt for socks every Sunday morning. Maybe they will come whenever the family goes to someone's home for a visit. Parents should anticipate and instruct their children in preparation for these times—whether it is Saturday night, or in the car on the way to a friend's house.

A Short Biblical Reference List

What does the Bible say about obedience in general? "Children, obey your parents in all things, for this is well-pleasing to the Lord" (Col. 3:20). It also says "Honor your father and mother, that your days may be long upon the land which the Lord your God is giving you" (Exod. 20:12).

What about anger? "He who is slow to wrath has great understanding, but he who is impulsive exalts folly" (Prov. 14:29). And again in Proverbs (which incidentally is a wonderful book for parents): "He who is slow to anger is better than the mighty, and he who rules his spirit than he who takes a city" (Prov. 16:32).

What passages can a parent use when the child is being urged to confess sin? "He who covers his sins will not prosper, but whoever confesses and forsakes them will find mercy" (Prov. 28:13). The same thing is taught in the New Testament. "If we confess our sins, He is faithful and just to forgive us our sins and to cleanse us from all unrighteousness" (1 Jn. 1:9).

Suppose a child is guilty of envying another child. "A sound heart is life to the body, but envy is rottenness to the bones" (Prov. 14:30). And James tells us,

> But if you have bitter envy and self-seeking in your hearts, do not boast and lie against the truth. This wisdom does

> not descend from above, but it is earthly, sensual, demonic.
> For where envy and self-seeking exist, confusion and ev-
> ery evil thing will be there. (Jas. 3:14-16)

Another common problem, particularly with boys, is laziness. "The hand of the diligent will rule, but the slothful
will be put to forced labor" (Prov. 12:24). And Paul says,
"For even when we were with you, we commanded you
this: If anyone will not work, neither shall he eat"   (2
Thes. 3:10).

Lying is a common problem with children. "Do not
lie to one another, since you have put off the old man
with his deeds, and have put on the new man who is renewed in knowledge according to the image of Him who
created him . . ." (Col. 3:9-10). And Solomon teaches us
that "the truthful lip shall be established forever, but a
lying tongue is but for a moment" (Prov. 12:19).

Children have not been alive very long before they
discover the pleasure found in letting someone else have
it. They learn how to call names. But Jesus said,

> You have heard that it was said to those of old, 'You shall
> not murder,' and whoever murders will be in danger of the
> judgment. But I say to you that whoever is angry with his
> brother without a cause shall be in danger of the judgment.
> And whoever says to his brother, 'Raca!' shall be in dan-
> ger of the council. But whoever says, 'You fool!' shall be
> in danger of hell fire. (Mt. 5:21-22)

Stealing is not limited to bank robbing and shoplift-
ing. More than one child has come home from a friend's
house with some little thing clutched in a tiny little fist.
"You shall not steal" (Exod. 20:15). And children should
also be taught the importance of restitution:

> Speak to the children of Israel: 'When a man or a woman
> commits any sin that men commit in unfaithfulness against
> the Lord, and that person is guilty, then he shall confess

the sin which he has done. He shall make restitution for his trespass in full value, plus one-fifth of it, and give it to the one he has wronged. (Num. 5:6-7)

And of course, children prone to self-righteousness love to tattle. This is a sin which good children, children rarely needing discipline, love to commit. "You shall not go about as a tale-bearer among your people . . ." (Lev. 19:16). And Proverbs teaches us that "he who covers a transgression seeks love, but he who repeats a matter separates the best of friends" (Prov. 17:9).

The influence of such scriptural instruction can be profound. I can still remember two of my earliest lessons in Scripture, taught to me and my siblings by my blessed mother, through constant repetition. My mother was our faithful Moses as he spoke to the children of Israel in Numbers—"be sure your sin will find you out." And of course, I also learned (in King James) "be ye kind one to another, tenderhearted, forgiving one another. . . ." Such lessons last for a long time.

Disciplining Little Ones

God the Father is a good father to us. "As a father pities his children, so the LORD pities those who fear Him. For He knows our frame; He remembers that we are dust" (Ps. 103:13-14). As Christians we fear and honor Him; as we do, He remembers our frame. This text tells us that the Lord pities us and accommodates our frail capacity. In doing this, the Lord is like a good father, watching over His children. An important principle is demonstrated here, which parents should consistently remember and apply. We are taught that God *knows* our frame, He *remembers* that we are dust. In this, He is like a human father. So as we seek to be good parents, we must know our children's frame. "Fathers, do not provoke your children, lest they become discouraged" (Col. 3:21). This can only come about through carefully studying and considering our children. A special area of importance in this is considering how our children respond to us as we exercise disciplinary authority over them.

We forget our children's frame in different ways as we exercise authority. Some parents have gotten caught in the trap of *countless* rules. Taking their cue from some federal agency, they surround their children with a constant, bewildering stream of requirements. But when laws multiply, so does non-compliance. In contrast to humanistic law, God's law is plain, simple, and to the point. Humanistic law is complex, devious, twisted, contradictory, and endless. Rules in a godly house should therefore be *basic* and easy to understand. "You must always tell the truth. You must always obey us immediately. You must always respect your mother." This does not cover every situation, but it actually does come close.

Another problem is that of *unnecessary* requirements. Take the example of a mother with a toddler, visiting a friend's house. The child is happily playing. When it is time to go, the mother should not thoughtlessly create a showdown. "Come here. Put on your coat." If she gives a command which is disregarded, then discipline becomes necessary. Commands should therefore not be given thoughtlessly—thrown out in an offhand way. The mother will save herself a lot of grief if she just goes over and picks her child up. If at *that* point the child resists, discipline is fully appropriate and necessary. This is not catering to the child; it is simply a matter of picking the battles carefully. Multitudes of occasions will require swift and effective discipline. No home has a *shortage* of such times. So why create more such occasions than you really need?

Yet another problem occurs when parents unnecessarily *blindside* the kids with a requirement. For example, suppose the kids are playing outside after dinner, when one of the parents goes to the door, and calls, "Time to come in!" This is just asking for static. A better way is to give some advance warning. "Ten more minutes!" Then when they are called ten minutes later, there has been ample time for mental adjustment and spiritual preparation.

Another, very serious problem exists when parents exercise their authority over their children in a sinful way, and then (for the sake of "maintaining authority") refuse to apologize and make restitution. We can characterize this as the problem of *stubborn* requirements. One of the best ways to teach the sovereignty of God over the home is for the children to see the parents submit to God's authority in practical ways. This can occur in many areas, but one of the most important is through apologies offered to children by parents. This teaches the children that the requirements of the home are not the result of random neuron-firings in the parental brain—the requirements are given by God, and the parents are under that authority as much as the children are. A besetting sin of *anyone* in authority is the reluctance to confess sin for fear of jeopardizing their position. Parents must especially guard against this; so if you screwed up, say so.

There are times when a child should be disciplined, but in a situation when the parent is tempted to do so for self-centered reasons. But discipline is not to be done for the parent's sake, but rather for the sake of training the child. The child must be disciplined out of concern for him. If a child is disciplined because the parent is irritated, then he is being disciplined for the wrong reasons. Discipline for the right reasons is for the child's sake and not for the sake of the parents.

Some parents are hard on their children because that is the personality type of the parents. Some parents are soft for the same reason. But as Christians we must reject the implicit pagan determinism of "personality types." God charges us all with the task of being *wise* parents— no matter who we are. This means that when we take a hard line, we do so biblically and thoughtfully. And when we remember "the frame" of our children, we do so biblically and thoughtfully.

The results will be families which are honoring to God, and to the cause of the gospel. Our children will grow up in a home with high disciplinary standards, but those standards will not be burdensome. God says to us that "this is the love of God, that we keep His commandments. And His commandments are not burdensome" (1 Jn. 5:3). We should be able to say something very similar to *our* children.

Conclusion

Once parents have come to understand the Bible's teaching on the authority they have been given over their children to discipline them, this understanding, coupled with a knowledge of the nature of the child, creates a new urgency for the task of balanced and faithful discipline. The Bible identifies the refusal to discipline a child as the parents setting their hearts on the child's destruction. Now of course a Christian father certainly will never turn to his wife and say, "Honey, let's destroy our children." But those who do not discipline are *in fact* destroying their children. This is taught in Proverbs 13:24: "He who spares his rod hates his son, but he who loves him disciplines him promptly." According to the Bible, if the little ones are not disciplined, they are being treated with contempt and hatred. Suppose parents look with tenderness at their sleeping children and ask themselves, *Do I hate these small children?* The obvious answer is *no*, but if they are not disciplining them, the biblical answer is *yes*. The biblical assumption which therefore should undergird all child rearing is very straight forward: dad and mom are bigger than the children. If the children are doing something wrong and consequently self-destructive, *they must be stopped*. If the parents refuse to make them stop, for whatever reason, they are treating their children with contempt and hatred.

At the same time, child rearing is not doom and gloom. If children are disciplined well and seriously, it creates an opportunity for a great deal of joy in the home. God will give great joy in the family if the parents are in obedience to Him. Disciplined children are children who are *enjoyed*. Undisciplined children cannot be enjoyed by the parents. Enjoyment, peace, and order in a Christian home are the fruits of discipline. If child discipline is approached with all the appropriate seriousness, then there is going to be much room for joy, laughter, and fun because everyone knows the boundaries and respects them.

Parental authority is *ministerial*, delegated to the parents by God. This means that the parents' authority over their children does not rest upon the *size* of father and mother, or their superior strength, wisdom, intelligence, or age. If children are honoring their parents, they are in fact being obedient to God, not man. There are non-Christian homes where the father runs a tight ship, but the Word of God is not there. Just because the home life is disciplined does not mean that it is godly. Children should know that their father and mother are not the ultimate authorities in the home but are God's ministers who have a Lord above them. The children are to submit to their parents, and the parents are to submit to God. The children should be taught obedience to God *through* obedience to their parents.

The command, "Obey me because *I* said . . ." rests upon the parents' intelligence or strength. When the father and mother vest all the authority in themselves, it can be overthrown and removed if the child gets bigger and stronger than they are (or if he *thinks* he has). But if children are obeying God through obeying their parents, then that authority can never be toppled.

CHAPTER TEN

Miscellaneous Concerns

Planning Our Children's Future

> So the king of Israel answered and said, "Tell him, 'Let not
> the one who puts on his armor boast like the one who takes
> it off.'" (1 Kgs. 20:11)

As more and more believing parents are seeing the
bankruptcy of humanist practices in childrearing, they are
starting to reject the common Christian practice of mimicking the world in its childrearing. The world's practices
include such obvious things as discipline through time-
outs and grounding, education through government schools,
sexual seduction through recreational dating, and more.
Many Christians have quite simply had it, and they want
out. So far, good.

But biblical balance is a hard thing to maintain. The
more Christian parents find their way to declare war on
worldly parenting, the better it will be for all of us. But
some Christian parents have begun to beat spear upon shield
in an odd sort of way. It is one thing for a husband and
wife to resolve before the Lord what they feel called to
do in the task of parenting, but it is quite another to announce the *details* of that agenda, as though the thing were
as good as done, to a bystanding and bemused community.

Like anyone else engaged in difficult and demanding

work, parents ought not to be noisy about the *details* of their plans before they come to fruition, ought not to count chickens before they hatch, and ought not to disregard the apostle James.

> Come now, you who say, "Today or tomorrow we will go to such and such a city, spend a year there, buy and sell, and make a profit"; whereas you do not know what will happen tomorrow. For what is your life? It is even a vapor that appears for a little time and then vanishes away. Instead you ought to say, "If the Lord wills, we shall live and do this or that." But now you boast in your arrogance. All such boasting is evil. (Jas. 4:13-16)

If we are to remember that our lives are a mist when it comes to such mundane matters as business and making money, *how much more* should we be cautious and humble when it comes to the details of our children's future?

For an extreme example of this, many see that our common system of recreational dating is not at all biblical, and so they are returning to the concept of biblical courtship. But some are even going beyond courtship, and have begun to talk about arranged marriages. Even this is not necessarily a problem. There is nothing *necessarily* unrighteous about an arranged marriage. Abraham, for example, arranged Isaac's marriage through a faithful servant (Gen. 24:2-4). But when arranged marriages have honored God, it has been the result of parents taking full advantage of their maturity and wisdom. Older parents of young women, for example, can often see through the pretensions and bluster of the young suitors knocking at the door—and often with much more clarity than the object of all the attention does. But suppose that the parents are talking this way about arranged marriages, and making plans, when the future bride and groom are both six months old, and the parents are just a few years older than when *they* started dating. "Come now, you who say . . ." Not only are our lives a mist, but this truth that we are all wisps of cloud certainly includes our children. A few moments' reflection should show the *numerous* ways in which our fond early hopes concerning the children of close friends could be dashed. After fifteen years have passed, the diversities are starting to become apparent. One child is intelligent, the other is slow. One is gregarious, the other painfully shy. One is very pretty, and so is the other one. In short, time reveals much that wise parents should take into account in a question of such importance. But when the shoots first appear above the ground it is difficult for the horticultural layman to distinguish the peas and beans.

Certainly there is nothing wrong with parents publicly expressing their desire that their children walk with God throughout life. Indeed, the Bible *requires* parents to be quite visible in this commitment and desire. But the reason parents may be publicly committed in this desire is the fact that God has given many promises concerning this in His Word. God has promised that faithful parents may trust Him for faithful children. But God has promised us *nothing* about the godliness, intelligence, personality, graces, of someone else's six-month-old.

For another example, while we may trust God for the *character* of our children, He has not promised us anything about our children's intellectual capacities. Suppose parents have undertaken a rigorous program of homeschooling, or they plan to enroll their child in a world-class private Christian school. Having done so, they announce proudly to all their friends that their child is going to be a NASA scientist, or that he'll be reading the Greek New Testament by the age of four. Well, maybe. The best educators in the world cannot put in what God left out. "Come now, you who say. . . ."

Parents should set goals for their children, and then they should act in a way that is consistent with those goals. Such goals are certainly lawful. And, because interests vary widely, so will the goals. Some goals may be athletic, some musical, some linguistic, and so on. But parents must remember that, in all such work, they are utterly dependent upon the will of the Lord. And because His will in these things has not yet been revealed, it is very important to guard our lips in humility, and if we say anything, say, "If the Lord wills. . . ."

Insecurity in Daughters

Insecurity will be evident to attentive parents if they watch for it long before it manifests itself in disobedience. For example, little girls should have a very great aversion to strange men. If a little girl climbs up into a strange man's lap with no encouragement at all and is all over him like a wet towel, that little girl is headed for trouble. If she is not getting sufficient masculine attention at home from her father, she will start getting it wherever she can.

When I was a boy, my family went to visit some people who had a little girl. After the visit, when we were driving home, I remember my father saying to my mother, "They are going to have problems with her with men when she gets big enough." She did not know my dad very well at all, and she was way too friendly. She was not getting her security from her father. When a little girl does that she is a nuisance to men. But when she grows into a young woman, she has something to use, and males are not as reluctant to show her attention as they used to be.

If a father wants to protect his daughter from immorality, he must surround her with masculine security. It must be established in her mind that if anyone is going to marry her, he is going to have to measure up to her dad. A father should be able to look his daughter in the eye and say, "Honey, I don't care who you bring home as long as you respect him as much as you do me."

Provoke Not . . .

Colossians 3:21 states, "Fathers, do not provoke your children, lest they become discouraged." And in Ephesians 6:4 it says something very similar: "And you, fathers, do not provoke your children to wrath, but bring them up in the training and admonition of the Lord."

When the Bible singles out a particular class of people, and tells them to avoid something, then it is reasonable to suppose that this instruction has a *specific* relevance for that particular class of individuals. If fathers are told not to provoke their children to discouragement or wrath, there is a reason the *fathers* were instructed this way. Fathers have a temptation to provoke their children in a way others do not.

In comparing these two verses, it can be seen that the children are different. Some children are prone to rebellion—a provocation for them is to wrath. Others are tempted to crumple—a provocation for them is to discouragement. But in both cases, the father is the one responsible.

Generally, when fathers do not treat their children properly, the ones provoked to rebellion will usually be boys, and the girls will frequently be the ones provoked to insecurity and discouragement. Many fathers with daughters will say, "My girls are turning out fine." This is because they are not overtly rebellious—but an insensitive father may be blind to the discouragement he brings. An overbearing father can thoroughly discourage his daughters and never even see it.

In Ephesians, the alternative to this kind of provocation is not a lack of discipline. Some might say that if there is a danger of provocation from the father, then that father should not discipline. But this verse substitutes *bringing them up in the training and admonition of the Lord* for the sin of provocation. God tells the father to discipline instead of provoking. One of the reasons why fathers are frequently aroused to provoke their children to wrath or discouragement is because their children are out of control.

He comes home when the children are already wound up, tolerates it for twenty minutes, and then blows up. Because the children have to be told three or four times to do something, he is then tempted to provoke them. But if the children are well-disciplined and obedient, there is going to be no initial temptation for the father. But this can only come about if *he* is bringing them up in the training and instruction of the Lord.

CHAPTER ELEVEN

And When They Are Older . . .

Introduction

Parents who seek to honor God in their parental responsibilities must become accustomed to people telling them things about their responsibilities which are simply not true. This is true at every age-level—"Just wait until the terrible two's!"—but the pleasure many take in dire prophecy does not cease just because children are approaching the teenage years. It is therefore important for parents to remember that the teenage years are *not* a time of innate and necessary rebellion. Many have assumed and taught that this is a time characterized by a necessary animosity between parents and children. This is simply false. However, if it is assumed to be true, it will be a self-fulfilling assumption.

If this is understood, there is no need to consider these years a time when one needs to call in the "experts." God expects children to be reared by their own parents, and in His Word, He has equipped these parents for the task. The teenage years are not a time for parental abdication—but these years do present an exciting challenge.

Loving Teenagers

As we should all know, the second greatest commandment is to love our neighbor. But who is our neighbor? As the parable of the Good Samaritan tells us, our neighbor is the one God has placed in our path, regardless who that one is. Consequently, there is a high priority placed on loving the neighbor within your home (1 Tim. 5:8). The commandments of God are not lifted or set aside in the home; rather, we are to make doubly sure they are applied in the home. After all, these are the people who are placed in our path every day.

It is easy to forget that our family members are our neighbors, and that we are consequently commanded to love them as ourselves. In addition to the forgetfulness of familiarity, there are some special reasons why it is easy to forget the requirement when it comes to our teenagers. Teenagers, unlike infants and young children, are not as naturally *lovable*. Consequently, because they can appear nerdish, ungainly, pimply, or whatever, some parents are less likely to give them the natural affection they received when they were little. This temptation must be strongly resisted. Also, because teenagers are bigger and smarter, loving them seems much more *complicated* than loving them used to be. So many parents just let it go. Loving them is harder, but it is a job to which parents are still called. Moreover, half of them (the girls) have turned into young women. Consequently, many fathers back off from giving physical affection through hugs, *etc*. But they need this affection very much. Because they appear much more responsible than they actually are, many parents take the shortcomings of their teenager *personally*. It may look like this particular act of irresponsibility was a deliberate affront, and it was not. It still requires discipline, but there is no need to take it personally as a deliberate insult.

Teenagers are much more independent than they used to be (they drive *cars*), so many parents assume that their teenager does not have the same need for love and affection he had when he was little. Now obviously, the means for showing such affection will change. If a mother's boy is now six foot three, the time for cuddling on her lap is long past. Still, this only changes the way affection is shown, not *whether* it is shown. Normal teenagers are young enough to be insecure, and old enough to hide it effectively. So it is important for parents not to believe what they say, or how they act, regarding this subject. Loving them should be obedience before God, and not a response to any requests made by them.

Teaching Teenagers

"The fear of the Lord is the beginning of knowledge, but fools despise wisdom and instruction. My son, hear the instruction of your father, and do not forsake the law of your mother; for they will be a graceful ornament on your head, and chains about your neck" (Prov. 1:7-9). Teaching teenagers is the responsibility of parents. As these passages make clear, parents are responsible for the instruction of their children—in *everything*. This does not mean that the parents have to do all the instructing; it *does* mean that the parents are held responsible by God for all the instruction. Nowhere in the Bible is the responsibility for a child's primary instruction assigned to the other two governments established by God—it is given neither to the civil government, nor to church government. This responsibility belongs to the parents.

The fact that parents need to instruct their teenagers means that teenagers have a need to *be* instructed by parents. In many dating situations, for example, if a young couple is asked what their parents think of their relationship, the reply reveals abdication on the part of parents—"they said, 'whatever you want.'" Teaching teenagers, however, is tricky on two counts. First, they in fact have a *greater* need for instruction than they have ever had before, and secondly, they assert that they have *less* need for instruction than they ever did. So whom do you believe? The truth or your teenager?

First, the teenage years will enable parents to identify much more clearly whether or not their child is exhibiting the fruit of regeneration. *Parents must not kid themselves.* An unregenerate sinful nature begins to appear in its true colors during these years, and in such a situation parents often have to work very hard to persuade themselves that their child is truly regenerate. Oftentimes, the weight of the child's eternal salvation is made to hang on a very slender thread indeed. "William was baptized as an infant—he must be regenerate." "Susan went forward at that revival three years ago—she's a Christian isn't she?" In both cases, not necessarily.

Teenage children should understand the radical nature of the depravity of sin, and they should thoroughly understand the remedy set before us in the gospel. They should understand this as having *direct* application to them. Christian home or not, by nature they are sinners. Christian school or not, by nature they are sinners. Homeschooled or not, by nature they are sinners.

Now of course, the gospel applies to *everything*. Those who make such an application have a Christian worldview. Those who do not make such an application may of course be saved, but they do not *think* like Christians. One important area is that of sexual responsibility. This necessarily goes beyond the "facts of life" talk. Such facts are of course included in the parental instruction, but parents are responsible for them finding out everything they need to know to serve God as a husband or wife—

> Oh, that you were like my brother, who nursed at my mother's breasts! If I should find you outside, I would kiss you; I would not be despised. I would lead you and bring you into the house of my mother, *she who used to instruct me*. I would cause you to drink of spiced wine, of the juice of my pomegranate. (Song 8:1-2)

In this book, we have frequently cited Deuteronomy 6:4-9. In that passage, we see a good setting for teaching teenagers. The best teaching time for your kids will be found to occur *in talks*. Fathers are not preachers, they are *fathers*. Mothers are not lecturers, they are mothers. This means that teenagers should be getting information from their parents on a constant basis—as they drive, as they walk, as they watch television, *etc. Parents must talk, and they must do so in the light of the Word.* The prime time for teaching is not in the midst of discipline, although that is when parents feel most like teaching. The best teaching times are when the children are not in trouble for something or other.

House Rules and God's Rules

It is very important for parents of teenagers to maintain the distinction we made earlier between house rules and God's rules. A great deal of damage is done when kids grow up in a Christian home where biblical law and house rules are confused. The bad will drive out the good, the traditions of men will replace the commandments of God— with moralism as the result. The result can be grown children who are aghast at the drinking of beer, but who tolerate gossip as a matter of course. But God never prohibited the former, and He strictly forbade the latter. What biblical parents want is morality, not moralism. *Begin by teaching this distinction to your teenager.*

Incidentally, this distinction will help solve one of the more common problems in dealing with teenagers—that of other Christian homes where that which you have forbidden is permitted. If the discrepency is over a question of biblical morality, then you should go to that other family in order to confront them. But commonly, the discrepency is caused by different families seeking to apply God's rules in a different way. A lack of wisdom *can* be evident here, but this sort of infirmity is not the same thing as disobedience and rebellion. Parents should encourage their children to "let it go" with their friends, and maintain their own house rules.

The distinction can be applied in many different

areas. In the area of hard work, we can see that one of God's rules requires hard work. One of the ten commandments requires a lifetime of labor, six days a week (Exod. 20:8-10). A teenager will be prepared to obey this command, or not, depending upon how he has been required to work in his home while growing up. But the variation in house rules applies directly to the question of work. Different families will place different emphases on how to train workers, and on what sort of work is more important to them. For example, there may be a choice between household chores, outside wage-earning jobs, or school-work. The measurement of success is seen in the fruit of instruction. Success is manifested in hard-working kids, and failure is evident in laziness and the shirking of responsibility.

Another area where house rules vary is seen in entertainment standards. Setting good work standards will solve a lot of this problem, but standards still have to be set. Low standards in entertainment can be the result of boredom, which demands to be entertained. A good way to solve the boredom problem is through work.

God's rules require that we not feed on that which is vile (Phil. 4:8; Eph. 5:3-4, 12). Parents should take care that they do not allow their children to be entertained by people they wouldn't allow into their homes. It is odd how many of us put up with language which would be intolerable if it were not coming from an electronic box. While house rules in different homes may vary (*i.e.* choosing movies that have different ratings), it is important to remember how sensitive the parents must be, how informed they must be, and how they must be *teaching* on what is seen. In the area of entertainment standards, parents are successful to the extent that they have taught their children to be sensitive to fine distinctions between good and evil (Heb. 5:13-14). Failure exists when the parents and children are insensitive to subtle moral distinctions, and the insensitivity exists because they have allowed those sensitivities to be bludgeoned into a stupor.

Another question concerns dress and hair standards. With regard to God's rules, the principal things to avoid are effeminacy in young men, and masculinity in young women. In addition, it is important that slovenliness and uncleanliness be rejected (Deut. 22:5; Num. 19). Now the house rules on such things should not be arbitrary—they should be seeking to put into practice what God has revealed. The Bible does not have anything to say about cultural variations, but this does *not* mean that it has nothing to say about cultural deterioration. On questions of dress, success should be measured by the teenagers' resistance to peer tyranny, and failure is seen when teenagers are slaves to such pressure.

Yet another area concerns standards of friendship. God's rules are clear on the subject. 1 Corinthians 15:33 says that "Evil company corrupts good habits." Notice that something is being *undone* here. Good habits were once instilled, and evil companions take them away. Many parents have not been at all slothful in what they have done—they have not left things undone. But they have been negligent by allowing *others* to undo their work. Again, house rules may vary. Some parents may see to it that their teens have no contact whatever with fools. Others parents, equally wise, may see to it that all contact occurs on the parents' terms. But parents who let their children run with the pack without any careful oversight have walked away from an important resonsibility. Success is seen when parents maintain shared values with their children, over against the values of young people who despise God. Failure is seen when the wisdom of "friends" is valued over the wisdom of parents.

"Let each be fully convinced in his own mind" (Rom. 14:5b). The Bible makes room for house rules. This instruction from Paul comes in the context of settling a dispute in the church about eating vegetables and observing special days. But the principle here merits our close attention because the modern church has more than her share of "debatable matters." Unfortunately, the fact that we have many opportunities to apply Paul's instructions does not mean that we necessarily *do*. Many of the debatable areas concern our teenagers.

The Bible does *not* teach, "There is no answer on these debatable issues, so leave the other guy alone." Consideration and courtesy are not relativistic. There *is* a correct answer. Paul, for example, gives us the right answer on the vegetarian issue, but also says that those who know the right answer are to defer to the weaker brother's conscience. The strong are to defer to the weak. So Christians have the right, according to Scripture, to eat only vegetables. They are to be left alone in God's house if they eat only vegetables, even though God calls it a weakness. Now if someone becomes imperialistic and insists that everyone *else* eat only vegetables, the clear duty of the church is to oppose such legalism. In Colossians, Paul requires us not to submit to decrees which say we are not to handle, taste, or touch (Col. 2:20-22). Christians must *not* obey the legalist. But if a weaker brother (or simply a brother with whom we differ) is applying this standard to himself alone, or to his own household, then we are to *leave him alone.*

Teenagers must know this distinction. House rules vary from one household to another. What does the Bible say about parents letting their daughters wear makeup, or letting them get their ears pierced? *Nothing*. It gives the authority for such decisions to the parents. Christian parents are free, in their own household, to say they would prefer their daughters not to wear makeup until they are grown. Others may let their daughters wear makeup in junior high. Isn't it wonderful how God has given different daughters to different families? We must all constantly seek to observe that great Pauline principle—*mind thine own business.*

To some, these issues may seem fairly trivial. But the

principle is not trivial, and we need to master it in such
simple situations. If we don't learn to practice it in the
little things, then we are going to see fellowship disrupted
over those issues which seem more important to us, but
which are still in the category of debatable matters. More
important, if we learn to distinguish between house rules
and God's rules when dealing with other families, we will
be able readily to maintain the distinction in our *own* homes.
We will be able to tell the difference between the prohibition of lying and the prohibition of jumping on the couch.

So if a biblical passage is brought to bear on a particular situation, the teenager is being instructed in the Word
of God. There may be some house rules that disappear as
a result of this. The judicious use of house rules that are
not in the Bible should be clearly identified as such. When
the chores are to be completed, or the standard set for
table manners, should be understood as house rules. If
the specifics of such rules cannot be backed up biblically,
then the parents should not apply them in the same way
they would if their child were caught in some act of
rebellious sin. Now of course, direct disobedience of a
house rule is a violation of God's rules (children, obey
your parents). But the distinction should nevertheless be
made and maintained.

Recovering Lost Ground

In many respects, child-rearing resembles other aspects
of life; just when a person has it all figured out, he is all
done. Many parents begin to learn about the basics of child-
rearing after their kids are older, and bad habits are
already firmly established. Therefore, we must remember that, with regard to forgiveness, God picks us up where
we are, not where we should have been. With regard to an
undisciplined teenager, God may use you to salvage what
may be salvaged. In some cases, tragically, it is may be
very little, while in others, a great deal may still be done.

Always keep in mind the distinction between *principles* and *methods*. Because every teenager is different, solutions cannot be mindlessly applied as though they were a magic formula. With a young teenager, parents may be able to do more. With a rebellious seventeen-year-old, parents may have to settle for less.

The first problem area is with sins of omission. These are the things a parent wishes the teenager would learn to do on his own, but that he does not seem to be able to grasp. The single biggest problem that parents have with this kind of thing is illustrated in Proverbs 19:19: "A man of great wrath will suffer punishment; for if you deliver him, you will have to do it again." Why does an undisciplined teenager do "whatever it is" over and over and over again? It is because indulgent parents cover for him, over and over and over. Parents will often sinfully indulge a rebellious teen through "picking up the pieces" for him. This is particularly difficult for many parents to learn, because they can easily be manuvered into feeling guilty by a manipulative teenager.

Here is the basic principle which should be *burned into the parental mind*. The parents' support and subsidy of their teenager should only go as far as their authority goes. Total subsidy means total authority, partial authority means partial subsidy, and so forth. An irresponsible teenager who is trying to "work the system" will want total subsidy and no authority over him. Parents who go along with this kind of thing will live to regret it.

But there are other problem areas as well (sins of commission). This can be seen when a parent is unable to tell his teenager to do something (say, clean the garage) without having a major confrontation over it. Here are a few things to remember:

1. Pick your battles carefully, and prayerfully. Many parents have a problem with this because they issue commands frequently and thoughtlessly.

2. When the battle is chosen carefully, it is of paramount importance to win that battle. If parents have already lost a great deal of ground, they will never recover it through losing *more* battles. So having picked the battle carefully, *do not lose*. One of the things the parents are seeking to re-establish is the respect the teenager should have for them. This cannot be done through vacillation.

3. If the situation is serious, the parents should avoid *any* battles over house rules, concentrating entirely on violations of God's rules.

4. But even when the enforcement is only of God's rules, it is important to maintain a sense of biblical perspective. Recognize that certain moral questions are very important indeed, and other biblical requirements are less important. If there is to be a confrontation, it should be over the most important issues, not the least important.

5. Parents should be seeking to establish a pattern of godly discipline. After one successful encounter, prayerfully seek another, and then another. It is worthless to have a successful disciplinary event that goes nowhere.

Leaving and Cleaving

> Now it came to pass, when Jesus had finished these sayings, that He departed from Galilee and came to the region of Judea beyond the Jordan. And great multitudes followed Him, and He healed them there. The Pharisees also came to Him, testing Him, and saying to Him, 'Is it lawful for a man to divorce his wife for just any reason?' (Mt. 19:1-3)

Some of the best information about the nature of marriage comes to us in the biblical teaching about the dissolution of marriage—divorce. In this passage, Jesus is tested with a question about divorce. In order to understand His response, we must realize that the question sprang from a specific context. Two schools of thought on divorce were in place among the Jews of that day. One school held that divorce was only permitted for specified biblical causes; the other that divorce could be obtained for any and every reason. The Pharisees were asking Jesus to take sides in this debate. He responded that it was not legitimate for a man to divorce his wife for any and every reason. But in this response, He does not appeal to the teaching of one rabbi against another, He appeals to Genesis and the creation order.

In Genesis, God had a set purpose for creating man both male and female. They were to be no longer two, but one. When a man leaves his father and mother, marries a woman and becomes physically one with her, God unites them *covenantally*. Marriage does not occur whenever a sexual union takes place; it occurs when a sexual union is sealed with a covenantal oath. In his first letter to the Corinthians, Paul says the "one flesh" aspect of a sexual union takes place even if it is an illegitimate union with a prostitute. Sexual immorality involves the blessed sexual union in immoral activity—activity prohibited by the law of God. This "one flesh" union does not bring about a marriage. In His teaching on divorce, Jesus quotes this passage emphasizing the nature of the covenantal union. A man leaves his family, his parents let go, and a new family is formed. In Eph. 5:25-33, Paul states that this leaving and cleaving is a profound mystery; he also emphasizes the union in order to show that the union is a picture of Christ and the church.

The Bible requires children to honor their parents throughout life. When they are little this honor takes the form of *obedience*. But this obligation to obedience ceases when a new household is formed. If a boy were to obey his parents all the way through life, there is no way he could really leave them, cleave to his new wife, and establish a new household. When a man cleaves to his wife, she also leaves her family and the authority over her is transferred from her father to her husband.

A problem exists when women in submission to their husbands seek to remain in submission to their fathers. If a man and woman do not *leave* their parents in order to start a new family unit, considerable difficulties will arise. With regard to authority, the parent/child relationship does not have the same permanent status as does the husband/wife relationship. Of course the parents must always be honored, and the parents should always love their children. But the authority relationship between husband and wife is a permanent one—it cannot be dissolved without sin *somewhere*; the relationship with sons and daughters is not permanent in the same way.

When the children are little, the parents are supposed to make decisions to control and protect their children. When the children are ready to marry, the parental responsibility goes in the opposite direction—it requires the parent to grant the child the liberty to leave and form a new primary allegiance. This is oftentimes difficult because the wiser the parents are about life, the more tempted they will be to violate this principle. But this must be remembered: parents who have young children have many years before marriage to instill those values. They must instill these values at a young age so the decisions made by their older children are second nature, made without verbal reminders from concerned parents. Children should leave home and make their own mistakes. If they have been brought up well, those mistakes will not be horrific.

The parents should view themselves as successful if their seventeen-year-old boy *wants* to be away from home. Loving and protective parents are going to be tempted to feel hurt if he does not want to be with them all the time, but God did not create him to stay at home. If this principle is neglected, many family problems can ensue. For example, problems can be caused when parents and grown children stay in the same house, or when they live too close together. Of course, this does not mean a couple cannot visit the folks at Christmas for a week, but married couples know that even doing *this* can cause troubles. For example, who's in charge of the grandkids now?

The newlyweds must make sure they have left their parents both externally and internally. The lines of authority *must* change, but the honor, respect, and fellowship must not diminish. Before they leave the nest, children are required biblically to render honor to their parents by obeying them. After they leave, they should honor their parents through expressions of respect.

This means godly parents should not require as much of their child when he is older and still under their roof as they do when he is younger. This is simply intelligent anticipation. They have the *authority* to tell their teenager what to do, but they should use that authority by preparing the child for the day when they will not have the authority. So they should not tell their teenager what to do in every detail—they want to prepare their child for leaving.

After the child has left, he still honors his parents by respecting them and by supporting them financially when they are older (Mk. 7:11-13). This may involve taking them into the home to care for them. Of course, there are certain situations where it is medically impossible to have elderly parents live in the home. But in a godly society, with a godly family order, the *common* practice of placing elderly parents in old folks homes would not exist. The proliferation of these emotional hellholes where people go to die, and where they spend the last fifteen years of their lives in lonely isolation, is an *abomination*.

CHAPTER TWELVE

Epilogue

Problem Children

We have all seen countless examples of the problem. Two tables away at a restaurant some little kid flips out. He doesn't like the kind of drink that was ordered for him. Attempts to quiet him don't work and finally his frustrated parents order him one of everything. Some of the kids down at the junior high amuse themselves by standing on the corner, yelling obscenities at passing motorists. A popular new evangelical pastor at a metropolitan church has a teenage son with hair down his back, a nose ring, three tattoos, and a bad attitude. When asked about his son's spiritual condition, the pastor just shakes his head. "You do everything you can," he says. The questioners nod sympathetically.

Parental Responsibility

The Industrial Revolution gave us far more than machinery and cheap textiles. One of the results of coming into a "scientific age" was the birth of the notion that "experts" were now needed everywhere. Everything became fair game for centralizers and planners, including the work of the home. The problem, however, was that the experts in the area of child-rearing and development were not qualified to teach according to Scripture, and their teaching consequently was not grounded at all in Scripture. They were self-appointed "experts" nonetheless, and their inane observations about children began to fill the country. And whether it was in response to Dr. Spock discouraging the spanking of disobedient children in the home, or Horace Mann and John Dewey building the Great Kidnapping Machine that we still call "public schools," parents began to acquiese, feeling as though they were not equipped to bring up the children God gave them. After all, they were not experts.

But the central problem was *not* that others offered to take over the rearing of children; the central problem was that parents disobeyed God, and let it happen. And because Christian parents abdicated, for a number of generations their children have suffered heavy casualties.

Outside the church, critics have observed the mess the family is in, and so they have begun to argue for a necessary abandonment of the "traditional family." Single parent homes, sodomite parents, child divorce, and day care centers are all offered as legitimate options among many. But such perversity is not really an abandonment of the traditional home; the traditional home disappeared a long time ago. These are merely attacking the vestiges. All this is merely the logical outcome of a disobedience that began a long time ago, in the last century, and is bearing bitter fruit now.

Within the church, we have countless youth ministries that have no idea that they are simply mimicking the world. Hedonism is thought to be an acceptable worldview for Christians if they are under eighteen; it only becomes false doctrine *later* in life. A glance at the ads for Christian colleges demonstrates beyond all question that the Christian church has generally accepted the Fun Imperative. When Christians are fighting for the family at all, they are fighting a defensive rear-guard action—fighting the more egregious symptoms (like child porn), and not the lies and distortions that brought the crisis about. We must not attempt to heal the wound of the people lightly. We must not say peace when there is no peace. In our reformation, and in our repentance, we must go to the root of the matter. Children must be brought up according to the Word of God, and according to *nothing else*.

The Reformation of the Home

The first place where this reformation must come is in the area of the requirements the church places upon her elders and deacons. The Scripture requires that church officers manage their homes well, and requires that the children of church officers be believers. The officers of the church are placed by God in a position to be examples to the congregation. The members of the church are commanded to imitate them, carefully considering the outcome of their way of life. This way of life includes the very important matter of how they bring up their children. There will be no reformation and no revival until those pastors who do not meet the child-rearing qualifications of their office step down, in repentance, from their office. Men who have a household in disarray are just as unqualified for church office as a lesbian is. It is way past time for conservative Christians to cease being outraged with the disobedience of *others*. Why do we remove the beam from their radical eye when we have a telephone pole in our own conservative eye? If the church permitted polygamy among the elders, then the households of the membership would be in shambles as well. Such disobedience cannot produce good fruit. We are guilty of such disobedience, and we must not be astonished at the results. There are, of course, other areas of childrearing which must be addressed as well. But unless this happens within the leadership of the church, all other efforts are futile. And when it happens, as it will, all other reforms will follow.

Two Roads

Parents in the fifties used to worry about their kids, but not in the same way contemporary parents worry about their kids. Kids used to rebel, sure, but not like they do now. Before the late sixties, the quest for teenage autonomy was a tame affair. It all seemed like a big deal at the time, but now in retrospect it looks positively *calm*. After all, parents used to think *Herman's Hermits* were radical anarchists.

But actually it all seemed like a big deal at the time because *it really was*. The human race may travel only one of two roads. One leads to eternal life and the other to eternal destruction. The first few steps down either road may not reveal the radical difference in destinations. But the fact that the roads may appear to be very similar at the start does not alter the final antithesis between right and wrong, righteousness and sin, heaven and hell.

This is why the rebellion of children should have mattered to parents in another generation *as parents*, and now should matter to us in the same way. We must consider the teaching of the Bible on the nature of generations. What we call a generation gap is really the fulfillment of God's promised blessings and curses on families. The Bible shows that these two roads—to life and to death—are usually traveled *generationally*. The Ten Commandments say that we may not bow down to gods other than the Lord. And why? "For I, the Lord your God, am a jealous God, *visiting the iniquity of the fathers on the children to the third and fourth generations of those who hate Me*, but showing mercy to thousands, to those who love Me and keep My commandments" (Exod. 20:5-6).

We do not like it this way, but the effects of individual choices cannot be contained within the boundaries of individual lives. As parents, the road we travel will always enable our children to travel further *down that same road*. When we see our children doing things which affront our values, the teaching of Scripture requires us to consider whether this is more a fulfillment of what we believe rather than a collision with what we believe. Are we looking at our children, or are we also looking at our *sin's* children? Perhaps some parents have spent time looking at their children's baby pictures—wondering how that cute toddler came to be, sixteen years later, so detestable in appearance. Why the pierced eyebrows and lips? Why the filth? Why the music that isn't? Why the deliberate and repeated attempts to insult everything the parents hold dear?

Parents who are not followers of Jesus Christ must understand that through their own unbelief they are leading their children in the most fundamental rebellion of all. Because this is the case, no room remains for objecting if the kids then take their initial rebellion into the final stages. Before reaching that final dead end, it is easy for an unbelieving parent to say that although he does not believe in Christ, yet he knows how to restrain himself (unlike these kids today). See, he stops *here*. But his children, and then his grandchildren, will wonder *why* he stopped there. It seems so arbitrary to them—it *is* arbitrary. "If Christ is not Lord," he might reason, "I don't have to do everything He says." The children take it farther. "If Christ is not Lord, I don't have to do *anything* He says." The result is ethical nihilism—nothing coheres, nothing has value, nothing *tastes*. It is very easy to look at these children— the children with hollow eyes—and assume the problems began with them. But this is not the case.

The children of our culture are growing up under the wrath and anger of God. His judgment on them is manifest in the insolent way they walk, the sullen look on their faces, the arrogant ignorance of their speech, the moral idiocy of their sexual lives. Clearly these children are hated and rejected by God—He has delivered them over to the suicidal pattern of sin. Why is God destroying them? The biblical answer is that their *parents* hated Him, and He is visiting that iniquity downstream. Because they are children of disobedience, they will die. The apostle Paul teaches that if neither parent believes in Jesus Christ, then the children are foul—unclean. They are displeasing to God. And many Christian parents have failed to cling to their covenantal promises and duties, and so they have lost their children.

Forgiveness is certainly possible—Christ came to save *sinners*—but this forgiveness is not for those who resist the justice of the judgment upon them. It is good and right for God to visit the effects of our sin on our children. In the context of God's anger at sin (and only there), forgiveness is offered by Christ to all who repent of their rebellion and believe in Him. It is not offered to those who complain about the negative effects of their rebellion. When the message of salvation comes to unbelieving parents, it is offered to them as parents. This means that they must *repent* as parents. If they do, He will always show mercy. Likewise, when the message of covenantal renewal comes to believing parents, mercy is always available.

> Behold, I will send you Elijah the prophet before the coming of the great and dreadful day of the Lord. And he will turn the hearts of the fathers to the children, and the hearts of the children to their fathers, lest I come and strike the earth with a curse. (Mal. 4:5-6)